30 PIECES OF SILVER
ISBN 1-886885-18-4

Published by Spirit of Life Publishing
27 West Hallandale Beach Blvd.
Hallandale Beach, Florida
33009-5437, U.S.A.
(954) 456-4420

www.JonasClark.com

01 02 03 04 05 06 07 ¨ 07 06 05 04 03 02 01

ABOUT THE AUTHOR

Jonas Clark is a refreshing voice and a champion in the contemporary church. Jonas served God for more than two decades as a pastor, teacher and evangelist before the Lord called him to his role as an apostle in the end time church.

An evangelist at heart, Jonas travels around the world preaching the Gospel with a bold apostolic anointing. Fortitude and God's grace have taken his ministry into more than 25 countries, where he delivers a message of salvation, healing, deliverance and apostolic reformation. His passion is to win lost souls for Jesus Christ and equip every believer to take the Good News into the harvest fields to fulfill the Great Commission.

Jonas is the founder of The Global Cause Network, an international network of believers and Champion partners united to build a platform for the apostolic voice. He also heads Spirit of Life Ministries, a multi-cultural, non-denominational church in Hallandale Beach, Florida.

Jonas is the publisher of *The Voice* magazine, a media platform for apostolic and prophetic believers.

Dedicated to my granddaughters

Alyssa Breanne
and
Kristianna Jordan

"Those who find Jesus, find all."

With love.

"Having a form of godliness, but denying the power thereof: from such turn away."
2 Timothy 3:5

CONTENTS

The religious spirit's purpose is to stand in the way of the Spirit of God's true work. It wants you to trade your liberty for legalism. If a religious spirit can't destroy your spiritual zeal, then it will try to conform you into its "respectable" image.

A religious spirit is a force that tries to get you to act pious, self-righteous or super spiritual. Before you can guard yourself from this spirit, you first have to understand what it is.

Religious spirits spend a great deal of time talking about what great and magnificent things they are going to do for God, yet seldom do more than criticize others.

Religious spirits try to become the church's "religious advisors" while infecting you with a spirit of discouragement. Through the eyes of a religious spirit, the local church is seen as a political ladder.

The religious spirit is dangerous with its words. Religious spirits can be most polite and enticing and engage you with flattering conversations. Beware, there may be a serpent behind those ruby red lips!

Pharisees, were teachers, interpreters and expounder's of the law of Moses, but they did not practice what they preached. Pharisees are strong examples of religious spirits.

Jesus is a loving shepherd, but He is also as bold as a lion when dealing with religious spirits. Let's take a look at some of the most severe words that Jesus ever spoke – the eight woes – and to whom He spoke them.

Maintaining a fervent prayer life is absolutely critical to advancing in your walk with Jesus. If you're lacking in this area, then you're already in spiritual trouble. Lukewarmness is the number one entryway for the religious spirit.

INTRODUCTION

The battle against the spirit of religion is one of the greatest challenges you face today as it opposes your ability to know Jesus for who He really is. Let's assume that you have been born again for 10 years. Certainly you should be more spiritually mature today than you were 10 years ago. Ask yourself this question: What enabled you to grow in your faith? You studied the Word, listened to many anointed Gospel messages, regularly attended church services, prayed daily, and walked through many fiery trials. But in reality, during that time of personal growth, it was your knowledge of Jesus that changed. You have no doubt experienced a greater revelation of His love for you and you see Him differently today than you once did. That's why the religious spirit is so dangerous. A believer can never grow beyond his or her understanding of Jesus.

Do you remember when Jesus asked His disciples, "Who do men say that I the son of man am?" They responded, "Some say that thou art John the Baptist: some, Elias; and others, Jeremiah, or one of the prophets" (Matthew 16). The people knew that Jesus was in a different class than anybody they had ever known or read about. But the greatest notion they could have of him was that of a prophet because there was nothing greater or more spiritual to compare Him to.

Then Jesus asked His disciples, "But who do you say that I am?" After a pause Peter spoke up and said, "Thou are the Christ, the son of the living God?" Peter's comprehension of Jesus was different than all of the others. His realization, however, would not go uncontested. Isn't it interesting that Peter faced great spiritual challenges in his life for declaring those words? The religious spirit came against him throughout his ministry. And Peter is the only one that Satan singled out and desired to sift like wheat. Peter is also the only one who walked on the water in the midst of a storm to come to Jesus. Peter was also the apostle that told the lame beggar at the gate Beautiful, "Silver and gold I don't have but such as I have I give unto you — rise up and walk." Was this because Peter's perception, image, faith, and understanding of Jesus was different? Did his revelation change his perception?

Why is it that so many people have so many different views of Jesus? Could it be possible that something unseen is molding their image of Him? As you read the pages of this book you will discover that religion corrupts a person's vision of Jesus. We cannot grow and mature beyond our comprehension of who Jesus is. That is why the corruption by the spirit of religion is so dangerous. Some see Jesus only as the baby in the manger. Others see Him continually hanging on a cross. Others see Him sitting in the midst of little children. Still others as a quiet gentle lamb. Yet there are many other descriptions of who Jesus really is. Yes, He is all those things but He is much, much more. He is the Lion of the Tribe of Judah, the Lord of Hosts, the Ancient of Days, the King of Glory, and even the Man of War.

This book will address some of the many ways that the religious spirit attempts to corrupt our understanding of who Jesus is. When we overcome the forces that challenge us we can grow beyond our current awareness of Him and become more like Him. Peter said, "Thou are the Christ, the son of the living God." Who do you say that He is? As you read this book, you may come to realize that your answer depends on how much the spirit of religion has affected you.

CHAPTER 1

A RESPECTABLE EFFIGY

The religious spirit's purpose is to stand in the way of the Spirit of God's true work. It wants you to trade your liberty for legalism. If a religious spirit can't destroy your spiritual zeal, then it will try to conform you into its "respectable" image.

Since I entered into full-time ministry many years ago, I have noticed that people manipulated by controlling religious spirits have most often been the ones that stand in the way of the Spirit of God's true work – reaching the lost, discipling believers and building strong local churches.

My heart particularly goes out to those that try to come to the Lord only to encounter a cold-hearted religious spirit that turns them away. I am also grieved for those who give their lives to the Lord only to unknowingly come under the influence of religious people that seek to change them into their own images rather than helping them grow and be conformed into the likeness of Christ.

Religious spirits like to mentor others and attempt to mold them into their own "respectable" effigy. The problem with that is the image of a religious spirit deceitfully appears righteous. Religious spirits are camouflaged by image. They are really full of hypocrisy, pride, false humility, self-righteousness, criticism, legalism and rebellion. An image is a...

face.

likeness.

model.

picture.

representation.

reflection.

facade.

illusion.

form.

Religious spirits are always into carnal form that has no genuine spiritual substance and quickly try to steal the zeal from newborn Christians in exchange for a facade that is nothing more than a religious form. There are many different tactics religious spirits use to impede the way of God's work. Tactics like obstructing the way of salvation, blocking the Holy Spirit's ministry, hindering the progress of the local church, or conforming you into a compromising believer.

The Spirit of God is actively pursuing those who are dedicated to advancing the Gospel, helping those who are born again to mature, building the glorious Church of Jesus Christ, and developing an intimate relationship with Him. Religion is actively opposing them.

TURNED AWAY

Sometimes religious spirits stand in the way of salvation. You may have heard stories about people that come off the streets and into the house of God only to be turned away by a self-righteous church member because of some legalistic dress code. Why would we turn away someone that was sincerely seeking the Lord? We spend thousands of dollars in our efforts to evangelize the nations, yet turn away some lost souls that willfully walk into the church for help just because they are not dressed "right."

How could something like this happen? Is it because the person did not measure up to some religious fashion? Could it be that the antagonistic church member was being influenced to act inappropriately by a

"We don't let that kind come into our church."

religious spirit? Could it be, just as Jesus taught, that the self-righteous church member did not know what spirit he was of? I wonder how many times a religious person has stood in the way of someone's salvation just because the poor lost soul was not conformed to its dignified image?

Of course, the religious spirit doesn't just impede the way of salvation, it also stands in the way of the Holy Spirit's ministry. I remember a newborn Christian that was pouring her heart out to God at the altar through her tears. Instead of finding comfort from a compassionate sister in the Lord, Mrs. Self-Righteous altar worker confronted her and accosted her habit of cigarette smoking. The altar worker told the baby Christian that maybe God might answer her prayers if she would quit smoking.

Granted, smoking will destroy your health and is a terrible witness, but was it really the time or place to discuss the bondage of smoking? Was what this religious spirit said even biblical? Moreover, why would someone interfere with the Holy Spirit who, Himself, was deeply ministering to this newborn? Was it simply a lack of wisdom on the part of this altar worker, or was she being influenced by a religious spirit that focuses only on the outward?

THAT KIND

Other times, religious spirits hinder progress in the local church. I know a pastor who reached out to different cultures in his city with great compassion. He understood the apostolic mandate to become a multi-cultural ministry (Mark 16:15). His desire was to break down the cultural barriers that existed in his territory. The pastor had discovered the strategy to reach his city – get out of the church and into the streets. As he began to work the area through evangelistic teamwork, the response in the new territory was tremendous. Hundreds gave their hearts to Jesus and many were baptized in the Holy Spirit. The lost and the unchurched were being reached and were on fire for God.

These new converts wanted to serve Jesus and began to come to church. It was refreshing to see their love for Jesus. To the pastor's absolute astonishment, however, he found himself engaged in a religious war with those long-standing church members that did not want to worship with "that kind" of people. Again, the new converts did not measure up to a laudable religious standard. In this example, the religious spirit was standing in the way of the pastor's work toward building the local church and equipping believers to do the work of the ministry.

As you can imagine, these self-righteous church members had created a religious stronghold in the church. Shortly after the pastor made several pleading attempts to convince this group of the importance of reaching everyone with the Gospel, the churches' board met together secretly and fired the pastor by unanimous vote. Could it be they were acting out of a religious spirit? The Word declares, "For he is our peace, who hath made both one, and hath broken down the middle wall of partition between us" (Ephesians 2:14). But instead of attempting to breakdown the walls of prejudice that divide the Body of Christ, religious spirits make it their mission to hinder the progress that would lead to a glorious Church without spot or wrinkle.

Ask yourself these questions:

Have you ever seen a religious clique form in your church?

Have you ever heard someone say, "We don't let 'that kind' come into our church?"

Have you ever seen someone hinder the growth of a believer or the local church?

Do you know a religious person who has the right religious image but lives a carnal life?

Have you ever seen religious people come together to strategize how to get the pastor to do what they wanted?

Has anyone ever insisted that you not pray so fervently?

Has a backslidden believer ever chastised you for your zeal for God?

THE FRUIT OF RELIGION

The fruit of the Spirit is love, joy, peace, patience, kindness, goodness, faithfulness, gentleness, and self-control (Galatians 5:22). The fruit of a religious spirit, by contrast, is self-righteousness, legalism, hypocrisy, a carnal view of Christianity, false humility, dead religious works, traditions, and instability. The purpose of the religious spirit is to stand in the way of God's work and corrupt your perception of Jesus. It does this with self-righteousness, false humility, dead religious works, vain traditions, and carnal focus. If the religious spirit can't discourage you spiritually, then it will try to conform you to its virtuous facade so that you will bear the fruit of religion instead of the fruit of the Spirit. For example, if you are on fire for God and praying effective fervent prayers that "availeth much" (James 5:16) then the religious spirit might try to get you wrapped up in praying nice, quiet "polite" prayers instead. Religion always tries to keep you quiet and if it is successful in its attempt to conform you to its nice, quiet, polite image, then you will lose your effectiveness as a Christian witness. The Holy Spirit doesn't inhabit anything that is bound in dead religious form. The Church of Jesus Christ is built on lively stones (1 Peter 2:5).

A RELIGIOUS SILHOUETTE

If its dead religious form does not stop you, then the religious spirit will try to take you out into spiritual bookie-bookie land, where you become so spiritual that you are no longer relatable. Many times I have met

The Holy Spirit doesn't inhabit anything that is bound in dead religious form.

people that were born again but they were so flaky and unstable that it was difficult to even hold a reasonable conversation with them.

It is the Holy Spirit's power and anointing that changes things, not a religious silhouette (Zechariah 4:6). Furthermore, the Word tells us of the anointing,

> "And it shall come to pass in that day, that his burden shall be taken away from off thy shoulder, and his yoke from off thy neck, and the yoke shall be destroyed because of the anointing" (Isaiah 10:27).

Religious spirits try to burden you down with a form of godliness while denying the power thereof so you will be ineffective in accomplishing God's plan for your life.

This same religious spirit will try to get you to take on this "godly form," while simultaneously challenging the reality of the Spirit of God in your life. Religious form always focuses people on the carnal, rather than the spiritual substance of the Word of God in a believer's life.

Like ice cream, religious spirits come in all different varieties and flavors. Some are religious about how you pray over your daily meals (very common). Others get hung up on what you wear to church. Still others are overly concerned with the formal and proper way to say, "Praise the Lord."

One of the religious spirit's main purposes is to get you off the mainstream of freedom and liberty that comes from the Spirit of Life into the legalistic bondage of form and liturgy.

Someone once said that the next move of the Holy Spirit is in liturgy. No way! Our God is a God of freshness, diversity and liberty. Our God is never boring. Jesus does not will for us to be influenced by a religious spirit. His will is for us to live by the law of liberty. Scripture says,

> "Now the Lord is that Spirit:
> and where the Spirit of the
> Lord is, there is liberty"
> (2 Corinthians 3:17).

There is freedom in the Lord, not religious bondage. Satan hates the freedom and the exciting life of the Spirit-led Christian. A Christian who walks in the Spirit is very dangerous to Satan and his kingdom because the Gospel is a divine invasion and attack against the powers of darkness. One of the most effective tools of Satan is to render the believers of God ineffective by creating religious people who are pious in form, yet without Spirit power. Again, Jesus is building His Church with lively stones, not dead ones. We can learn a lot about religious spirits by looking at how they behave.

SUMMARY
A RESPECTABLE EFFIGY

The purpose of the religious spirit is to stand in the way of God's work.

Religious spirits are always into carnal form that has no genuine spiritual substance.

Religious spirits like to mentor others and attempt to conform them into their own "respectable" images.

Self-righteousness and dead religious works are the fruit of religious spirits.

Religious spirits try to burden you down with a form of godliness while denying the power thereof so you will be ineffective in accomplishing God's plan for your life.

In the next chapter we will look more closely at what the religious spirit is.

CHAPTER 2

A DIFFERENT
SPIRIT

A religious spirit is a force that tries to get you to act pious, self-righteous or super spiritual. Before you can guard yourself from this spirit, you first have to understand what it is.

Some of you may have never heard of a religious spirit. Others of you may think being religious is a good thing, mistaking religion with right relationship with God. You may even ask, "What's wrong with being religious?" Or "So what if there are religious spirits? How can they affect me if I am a born again believer in Christ Jesus?"

In order to find truthful answers to these questions, let's look into what the Bible teaches about religion. First, exactly what is religion? Scripture says,

"Pure religion and undefiled before God and the Father is this, To visit the fatherless and widows in their affliction, and to keep himself unspotted from the world" (James 1:26-27).

So we learn from the above Scripture that religion in itself is simply...

to visit the fatherless and widows in their affliction.

to keep oneself free from worldly influences.

That sounds like a good thing on the surface – and it is. However, if we examine the sum of God's Word, we will soon discover that there is a religious spirit that is quite different from what the Bible describes as "pure religion." It is this different spirit that challenges our understanding of Jesus and endangers believers.

The Lord would not have us ignorant to the spirit of religion. The Bible gives us many examples of the operations of religious spirits throughout the Word including:

The scribes and Pharisees were ready to stone the woman who was caught in the act of adultery, yet there was no mention of stoning the man who was with her (John 8).

Apostle Peter and Barnabas would not sit and eat with the Gentile believers in Antioch when Jewish brothers came to visit from Jerusalem (Galatians 2:11-13).

The scribes and Pharisees challenged Jesus because His disciples did not wash their hands (ceremonially) before they ate (Matthew 15:2).

Jesus taught His disciples not to pray long prayers like the scribes, who prayed only for show (Luke 20:46-47).

Saul guarded the garments of religious murderers as they stoned a righteous man named Stephen to death (Acts 7:58).

After a notable miracle, a religious council, motivated by fear, reprimanded the Apostles Peter and John for speaking the name of Jesus (Acts 4:15-18).

> When Jesus healed a man on the Sabbath it so stirred up those with religious spirits they sought to kill Him (Mark 3:1-6).

We will examine many more examples throughout this book.

A DIFFERENT SPIRIT

Remember James and John, the two sons of thunder? They wanted to pray down fire from heaven on a Samaritan village because the people there would not receive the Lord. Upon hearing their request, our Lord responded harshly to His disciples: "You do not know what *spirit* you are of" (See Luke 9:52-55).

What did Jesus mean? A word study reveals the depth of the Lord's response. The Greek word for "spirit" is *pneuma*. From the word pneuma we derive the English word "wind." When we speak of the Holy Ghost, for example, we could also refer to Him as the Holy Pneuma or Wind.

In Samaria, a different spirit (wind or pneuma) was influencing the disciples. Notice also that Jesus made no excuses for James and John – they weren't just having a bad day – He was quite specific when He used the word "spirit." Again Jesus said, "You do not know what pneuma you are of."

But Jesus knew precisely what spirit the two disciples were of: a religious spirit. Religious spirits influence someone to act self-righteous. Self-righteousness means being filled with or showing a conviction of being morally superior or more righteous than others. It is important to understand that to be influenced does not mean to be possessed, but rather simply means to be...

affected.

inspired.

moved.

swayed.

motivated.

The disciples were outraged at the Samaritan's actions and began to act self-righteous because the Samaritans were not receiving Jesus, their Lord, into the territory. There is a difference between self-righteousness and righteous indignation. Can you imagine being so self-righteous that you are willing to call down the fiery judgment of God on an entire city? That's not normal behavior.

Jesus responded to the disciples' request with a rebuke. "But he turned, and *rebuked* them, and said, You know not what manner of spirit you are of" (Luke 9:55). To rebuke means to...

tax with a fault.

reprove.

censure severely.

admonish sharply.

PETER'S DIFFERENT SPIRIT

James and John were not the only disciples to be influenced by the spirit of religion. Peter, too, fell prey to this self-righteous spirit. If the spirit of religion could influence Jesus' chosen disciples, then none of us are immune. Let's study the Scriptures to gain insight into how the Apostle Peter was affected.

One day Jesus told His disciples that He would have to go to Jerusalem, suffer many things and be killed, but would be raised up on the third day. Peter took Jesus aside for a private talk and began to reprimand the Lord for saying such things. But Jesus was quick to respond to Peter and said, "Get behind me, Satan!" (Matthew 16:23) Like

James and John, Peter did not know what spirit he was of that day.

Jesus saw the influence of a different spirit (pneuma) at work on Peter that day and was very specific in rebuking Satan (the spirit) and not Peter (the person). Notice also that Jesus spoke directly to Satan, not an

The religious spirit did not disappear after the resurrection of Jesus.

attitude. The point of these two examples is to demonstrate three things:

1. It is possible to be influenced by a different spirit.

2. Jesus taught us to be aware of the operation of a different spirit.

3. It is possible to do something that looks religiously correct but could be done out of a wrong religious spirit.

INFILTRATING THE CHURCH

The religious spirit did not disappear after the resurrection of Jesus. In fact, the spirit of religion is an enemy that has always been around and is increasing its attacks against the Church. Believers need to understand the purpose of this spirit and why it is so dangerous. The mission of the religious spirit is to...

infiltrate your life.

bind your freedom.

steal your liberty in the Holy Spirit.

stop your advancement.

ruin your true Christian witness.

buffet the progress of the Gospel.

corrupt your perception of Who Jesus is.

SUMMARY
A DIFFERENT SPIRIT

A religious spirit is a force that tries to get you to act pious, self-righteous or super spiritual.

People influenced by the spirit of religion have an outward appearance of holiness, but are self-righteous in their innermost beings.

If the spirit of religion could influence Jesus' chosen disciples, then none of us are immune.

Believers need to understand the purpose of the religious spirit and why it is so dangerous.

Religious spirits will try to infiltrate your life and bind your liberty in the Holy Spirit.

In the next chapter we will take a look at the form of godliness that religion exhibits.

CHAPTER 3

A FORM OF GODLINESS

Religious spirits spend a great deal of time talking about what great and magnificent things they are going to do for God, yet seldom do more than criticize others.

With an understanding of the evil designs of the religious spirit, it becomes vital to recognize its characteristics so we can turn away from its influence.

In a letter to Timothy, the Apostle Paul warns his spiritual son about religious spirits and gives him implicit instructions about how to interact with them. Scripture says, "Having a form of godliness, but denying the power thereof: from such turn away" (2 Timothy 3:5).

As Paul so matter-of-factly points out,
religious spirits have a "form of godliness"
– they appear religious but lack the spiritual
substance of an intimate believer. Paul tells
Timothy to avoid such people – and with
good reason. Religious spirits sidetrack
people with the deceptive illusion of religious
form. Religious form is...

appearance.

structure.

ceremony.

formula.

liturgy.

ritual.

More interested in liturgy than liberty,
religious spirits are focused on outward
appearances. Religious spirits look at
things like the church building, the size
of the congregation, where the church is
located, and who is currently attending to
decide whether or not they want to be a
member of the assembly. They are always
more interested in form than what the
Spirit of God is doing among the people.
The result is that they miss the spiritual

dynamics of the church because of a focus on carnal externals.

Ask yourself these questions:

> Do you know anyone that chases religious status, titles and positions?

> Have you ever met a person that was offered a religious title or position in the church only as an obvious attempt to keep that person in the church?

> Do you know a person that acts like a know-it-all?

> Have you been around a person that projects an air of self-righteousness or a better-than-you attitude?

> Does someone expect you to do things that they are not willing to do themselves?

> Have you met the person who can't perceive the spiritual dynamics of the local church?

If you answered yes to any of these questions, then you have probably experienced the spirit of religion first hand.

THE HUNT FOR POSITION

Position seeking is one of the most obvious characteristics of the religious spirit. The religious spirit is always looking to advance into positions of influence and visibility in the church so that they can fulfill their purpose: to be admired of men. Since religious spirits are interested in status, titles and positions, they often choose a church based on whom they know that is already a respected member and what potential opportunities the pastor, or set man, will offer them to advance their own ministry. If they are denied the status, title or position they are seeking, then they often wind up church hopping in effort to attain their impure goals. Religious spirits want to know what is in it for them – how they can achieve recognition, visibility, position and honor within the local church – before they will commit themselves to the vision of the house. But these motives are contrary to the Word of God. Scripture declares,

> "Let me not, I pray you, accept any man's person, neither let me give *flattering titles* unto man.

For I know not to give flattering titles; in so doing my maker would soon take me away" (Job 32:21-22).

Titles, of course, are necessary because they help us define job descriptions and areas of responsibility in our society. To seek titles, however, with the intent of exercising religious control or to seek a leadership

Do you know anyone that chases religious status, titles and positions?

position to gain man's admiration is truly unrighteousness and is the activity of a religious spirit. Titles given only to flatter, manipulate or control someone are not biblical and ultimately lead only to confusion and trouble.

Sometimes titles are offered as a form of religious control. The disgruntled church member who is offered the title and position of a deacon by the pastor just to keep him from leaving the church. The evangelist that greets a pastor by preceding his name with a flattering and fashionable title in hopes of booking a meeting. These tactics simply feed the prideful nature of the religious.

I once met a man that was attending another church in our city. He was full of bitterness and resentment against his pastor and church and had developed a reputation for being a troublemaker by maliciously gossiping about anyone and everyone in the ministry. The man had become a religious critic. When this man announced his intention to leave the church in search of the perfect ministry the pastor ordained him as an Elder. This amazed me, considering the backbiting and gossiping the man had engaged in about both the church and the pastor. Was this man really ready for leadership? Was he really a good example to others of a Christ-like servant? Or was this simply a manifestation of religious control through flattering titles in an effort to keep this man and his money in the church? Perhaps you would agree that this man needed correction and not a position in the ministry.

KNOW-IT-ALLS

Besides seeking position, religious spirits are seldom teachable because they think they already know it all. Whether or not the religious spirit has ever had any actual first hand experience with the business at hand is of no matter. They may not have the first clue how to organize a banquet, for example, but they are quite sure that you are not doing it right and are even more certain that they could do a better job if they were only given the opportunity. It doesn't matter what the activity is, the religious spirit always thinks it knows more than you do.

This "know-it-all" attitude results in religious spirits becoming offended by anyone that they perceive may know more than they do. I speak from experience. Every religious person that ever walked into our ministry has made it clear to me that anything Minister So-and-So could do, he (or she) could do better. Surely we are always open to be taught, explore better strategies and ways of doing things but, unfortunately, most of the time a religious spirit's advice is only a facade for self-righteousness and criticism.

Ask yourself these questions:

> Have you met a religious person that was insensitive to the needs of those around them?
>
> Do those who labor among you do good things or God things?

Does someone you know always focus on your faults and continue to ignore your positive attributes?

Is someone critical of the way you do anything for God?

Have you ever been the victim of malicious gossip?

If you answered yes to any of these questions, then you have probably been the victim of the religious spirit.

PERFECTIONISM

What's interesting about a religious spirit is that even though they know it all they are often unwilling to jump in and help unless the task brings them some recognition. Religious spirits often tell you how to do what they are unwilling to do themselves.

One Saturday, we were in the park feeding the hungry and the homeless and sharing the Good News of Jesus Christ. After about 30 minutes, some people with religious spirits who were visiting from another city approached me and began to lecture me about what we were doing wrong. When they finally stopped, I simply asked them how much experience they had working with street people. Not surprisingly, they said they had no such experience. They had never fed, clothed or witnessed to the homeless, yet felt compelled to tell me that I wasn't doing it right. Notice that the religious spirit was unwilling to join in and help us feed the homeless and, in fact, had no prior experience in street ministry, yet expected me to change my methodology to suit their critism.

What's more, oftentimes a spirit of perfectionism accompanies a religious spirit. Perfectionism is an extreme behavior or expectation beyond the balance of being excellent. It is often non-practicable, extremely time consuming and because performance standards are raised so high the work never gets started, finished or measures up to the perfectionist's standards. That is why the religious perfectionist seldom accomplishes much beyond frustrating himself or criticism of others.

These same religious folks went on to tell me what we were doing for the homeless "was good but not good enough." Their point was that if we could not feed the people the way they would feed the people, then we shouldn't feed the people at all. One thing I've learned through the years of ministry is that if we had to do everything just perfect, then nothing would ever get done. I am not saying we should not maintain a standard of excellence in ministry. Yet, we should guard ourselves from the polarization of religious perfectionism.

When I looked at a hungry man eating the sandwich that we had just given to him, I had a hard time believing that it mattered

Sometimes titles are offered as a form of religious control.

to him how we presented the sandwich or the Gospel. I believe that God, however, was pleased with our effort to preach the Gospel and feed the hungry that day.

MANIPULATIVE

Religious spirits are notoriously hypocritical. Look no further than Judas Iscariot. One day at Lazarus' house, Mary anointed Jesus' feet with an expensive perfume (John 12:3-6). Some say that the perfume was made in Egypt and was very valuable. Well, Judas became very angry and terribly upset after watching Mary pour out the entire bottle of anointing perfume on the Master's feet.

Judas actually interfered and tried to stop Mary, saying, "Why don't we sell this ointment and give to the poor?" Sounds like an innocent idea, but it was not because Judas' motives were impure. It was a religious statement that Judas was really making with the intent to manipulate and control the situation. Scripture says,

> "Then took Mary a pound of ointment of spikenard, very costly, and anointed the feet of Jesus, and wiped his feet with her hair: and the house was filled with the odor of the ointment. Then saith one of his disciples, Judas Iscariot, Simon's son, which should betray him, Why was not this ointment sold for three hundred pence, and given to the poor? This he said, not that he cared for the poor; but because he was a thief, and had the bag, and bare what was put therein. Then said Jesus, Let her alone: against the day of my burying hath she kept this. For the poor always ye have with you; but me ye have not always" (John 12:3-8).

Judas' request was another characteristic of a religious spirit: control and manipulation. He was saying, "Let's do something good with the perfume, but let's not do anything for God with it." It's possible to do what appears as good works with wrong motives. Beware of good religious works and activities not motivated by the Spirit of God.

POLISHED

Religious spirits can be the most polite people (at least in public) you could ever meet. But remember this: words of deception, spoken with flattering lips, are still words of deception.

Religious spirits will continue to wear their suave facade until they find out that their smooth words are not effective in controlling or manipulating you. Then their tune will change, if you know what I mean.

If genteelness doesn't work, then the "God told me to tell you" line will often manifest. The problem is that God is always telling them that you should stick with their traditions and, of course, you had better listen! It is interesting to note that they always hear God speaking about your faults, but never exposing their own. Right!

Ask yourself these questions:

Have you encountered the religious person who can't take subtle hints of correction and make you spell it out in specific detail?

Is there anyone in your life who makes you feel like you are walking on eggs around them?

Have you ever been wrongly accused of being unloving?

Has anyone ever said to you, "And you call yourself a Christian!"

Do you know people who's perception of Jesus is limited to the baby in a manager or a little Lamb?

Have you ever met a person who wears their feelings on their shoulders?

Have you ever had a conversation with a person with a religious spirit who will not get to the point but makes you read between the lines?

If you answered yes to any of these questions, then you may have come into contact with the religious spirit.

"And you call yourself a Christian!"

CRITICAL

Back to feeding the hungry at the park, it seemed the religious folks had a never-ending laundry list of things they said that God told them about me and what I should do next time around to rightly accomplish my ministry work. I sometimes wonder if they thought it puzzling why God would talk to them about what I was doing without talking to me also? That, too, is just another characteristic of a religious spirit. Religion thinks that if God were going to talk to anyone it would be to him or her and not to you. The fact is that God had given us a strategy for feeding the homeless in our territory and we were obedient to follow His Spirit.

As we saw back in the park, religious spirits are downright obstinate. Religious spirits are always critical of the way you do anything for God. No matter how you do it, they will always tell you that it could be done better. Scripture declares,

> "And why beholdest thou the mote that is in thy brother's eye, but perceivest not the beam that is in thine own eye? Either how canst thou say to thy brother, Brother, let me pull out the mote that is in thine eye, when thou thyself beholdest not the beam that is in thine own eye? Thou hypocrite, cast out first the beam out of thine own eye, and then shalt thou see clearly to pull out the mote that is in thy brother's eye" (Luke 6:41-42).

Religious spirits rarely start or carry through on anything on their own accord. They will, however, talk about how poorly you do it. They spend a great deal of time talking about what great and magnificent things they are *going to do* for God, while simultaneously criticizing what you are *actively doing* for Him. Religious spirits like to talk the talk but fall short of walking the walk. In reality, they often do little outside of their own imaginations.

Watch out for the "but" statements from religious spirits because it's the springboard to critism. These religious folk in the park also advised us to open our homes to the people, something else that they were themselves unwilling to do. When I told them I felt that the Lord was probably laying it on their hearts to do just that, their response was, "No way would we invite 'that kind' of people over to our house." Can you see the hypocrisy in this? Beware of the critical religious spirit with an imagination ministry. Avoid the critics; work with the workers and not with the talkers.

GOSSIPS

Webster defines a gossip as "a person who chatters or repeats idle talk and rumors, especially about the private affairs of others." With such a critical nature, religious spirits find plenty to gossip about. Gossipy religious spirits are always looking for and talking about the faults of others. They are the ones with the beams in their eyes, but all they can see is the speck in yours (Matthew 7:3). People with religious spirits tend to look at themselves through rose-colored glasses, while looking at everyone else under a microscope. Gossip is the destructive weapon of the religious spirit.

Gossip is a marked characteristic of the religious spirit. They are critical talebearers and evil tattletales. You can spot gossipy religious spirits in the back of the church, hallways, bathrooms, and parking lots. Like birds of a feather that flock together, religious spirits hang out with, and are drawn to one another to assassinate others with their tongues. After church services, they can't wait to reach those telephones, online chat rooms and e-mails. The Apostle John wrote about the evils of gossip,

> "I wrote unto the church: but Diotrephes, who loveth to have the preeminence among them, receiveth us not. Wherefore, if I come, I will remember his deeds which he doeth, *prating against us with malicious words:* and not content therewith, neither doth he himself receive the brethren, and forbiddeth them that would, and casteth them out of the church. Beloved, follow not that which is evil, but that which is good. He that doeth good is of God: but he that doeth evil hath not seen God" (3 John 1:9-11, Italics added).

SNOOPS

Religious gossips will go out of their way to chase down rumors and pry into things that are surely none of their business in hopes of uncovering some juicy tidbit of information that they can use as a slanderous weapon.

One day a lady came to our church and within two short months she began to chase down a rumor about the marriage difficulties of a couple in the congregation that she didn't even know. She told anyone who would listen that one of the spouses was having an affair. As she launched her investigation she went so far as to call the church office in an effort to get a staff member to disclose more information about the couple's private affairs. The staff member discerned the evil motives and, of course, did not divulge any information.

To investigate, probe into, or to discuss the private lives of others is certainly way out of line. This woman actively pursued and dug for private information that was none of her business and that was an ungodly action. To make matters worse, this woman began to call others in the church to gossip and spread more rumors. No consideration or thought was ever given to the children of this couple or the fact that they were working together to overcome their marriage difficulties. Gossip is a sin that should not be tolerated. It is the fruit of a religious, self-righteous spirit. There is certain information that belongs only to God and the pastor. Let's keep it that way.

THE HYPOCRISY FACTOR

Never forget that religious spirits are hypocrites. Jesus wasn't kidding when He said that one should first remove the beam in his own eye. This gossiping church member had originally heard a rumor about this couple's marriage difficulty from another woman who was a member of a church in a totally different city. It just gets even more amazing doesn't it? This religious church member did not personally know this allegedly troubled couple, but stuck her big gossiping nose in these innocent people's lives. She had actually heard the ugly rumor from another woman in a far away place.

What can be worse than one gossip? Three gossips! Again, religious spirits are hypocrites. So where was the hypocrisy? The hypocrisy was that the church member spreading the prattle was getting her information from a woman whom was herself living in adultery. Because of the hypocrisy of a religious spirit, part of the lesson is that religious spirits often accuse you of having the problems that they have. Or they are often doing what they accuse another of doing. This woman, herself an adulterer, was accusing a young couple of what she was secretly doing.

INSENSITIVE

Religious spirits are insensitive. Another church group held an evangelistic outreach to homeless people in a park near their church. While speedily passing out tracts to as many homeless people as possible in 30 minutes, one believer was heard discussing plans with the group of eating at a particular restaurant for lunch in front of the homeless listeners. Should these believers have been more sensitive to having such a conversation within earshot of the hungry homeless?

Religious people are deceived by the "good work" of religious activity such as passing out a tract or a sandwich rather than seeking to produce life-changing results. Religion will focus on the natural activities and avoid the spiritual dynamics of serving Jesus, thus passing out the tract or sandwich and ignoring the spiritual need of the listener.

DECREE AND FLEE

Religious spirits don't take hints and cannot handle Spirit-led confrontations. Their motto is "decree and flee." They flee when exposed and decree how unloving and non-understanding you are as they go to the next unsuspecting pastor's church.

I have watched ministry leaders try to deal with and correct, ever so gently, these religious spirits to no avail. Religious spirits try to make you afraid to say anything to them at all because you never know how they may react. You feel like you're walking

Religious spirits are insensitive.

on eggs around them. Just go ahead and break the eggs because religious spirits can't take subtle hints; they must be confronted head on. Be humble of heart, without malice, innocent as a dove, gentle in your heart, but bold as a lion.

If you have made it this far in this book without getting upset, then you're doing pretty well. I once met a man that read this book and got so upset with me that he actually threw it in my face. I wonder what spirit (pneuma) he was operating in?

When you speak with truth and begin to expose a religious spirit, the person with the religious spirit may accuse you of being unloving and say that you are judgmental, full of hate, emotional, and non-Christ like. When confronted he may say things like, "You just don't understand me," or "And you call yourself a Christian!"

Many times I have seen them hide behind a religious facade called love. Love is the balance beam of Christians. It is the motivation of preaching the Gospel. It is the reason that God sent His only begotten Son into the world and offered Him up as the Lamb of God that taketh away the sin of the world. But love is not getting into agreement with some religious person's out-of-order flesh or nonscriptural critisms. Love should never motivate us to compromise our faith or the Gospel of truth.

The religious spirit is always stirred to accuse, when you speak out against apathy, traditions of men, and comfortable Christianity. He perceives Jesus as a little lamb never offending, upsetting or contending with anyone. But the Bible tells us that Jesus dealt strongly with sin. Scripture describes the day Jesus cleansed the temple.

> "And Jesus went into the temple of God, and cast out all them that sold and bought in the temple, and overthrew the tables of the moneychangers, and the seats of them that sold doves, And said unto them, It is written, My house shall be called the house of prayer; but

ye have made it a den of thieves"
(Matthew 21:12-13).

PUBLIC SPIRITS

Most of the time the religious spirits try
to appear righteous in public. They will say
things in front of others that tend to exalt their
religious posture or social status. Scripture
reveals the religious spirit's showmanship.

"And he spake this parable
unto certain which trusted
in themselves that they were
righteous, and despised others:
Two men went up into the temple
to pray; the one a Pharisee,
and the other a publican. The
Pharisee stood and prayed thus
with himself, God, I thank thee,
that I am not as other men are,
extortioners, unjust, adulterers,
or even as this publican. I fast
twice in the week, I give tithes
of all that I possess. And the
publican, standing afar off,
would not lift up so much as
his eyes unto heaven, but smote
upon his breast, saying, God
be merciful to me a sinner. I
tell you, this man went down
to his house justified rather

than the other: for every one that exalteth himself shall be abased; and he that humbleth himself shall be exalted" (Luke 18:9-14).

Religious spirits will speak of controversial subjects, and to be sure, at inappropriate times. They will take the Word of God out of

All the preacher
really wants is my money.

context to prove their religious points. I have actually watched religious spirits set up their Sunday school teachers, or other church leaders, to get them mad in front of others. The motive? To try to demonstrate that their composure (or rather religious smooth form) is proof that they have it all together and that you do not. Religious spirits will try to provoke you. Provoking is a weapon of the religious spirit that we discuss in greater detail in the next chapter.

VOICE OF A RELIGIOUS SPIRIT

I have come to quickly recognize the voice of a religious spirit. Perhaps you have heard his voice, too. He says things like, "You stand up too long in your church services. You take up too many offerings. That church music is too loud. Look at that jewelry; those earrings look demonic. All the preacher really wants is my money. You mean to tell me that sometimes your church services go past noon? Well, I would never go to that church with them acting like that. Look how emotional they are!" Perhaps you can think of some other statements from the religious spirit. Religious spirits hate emotion, with a passion.

Religious spirits attack emotion as "beneath" a good Christian's upbringing. Teach them in Greek and Hebrew, but don't you dare allow any spiritual punch or passion in your preaching or you will hear them say things like, "The Old Testament is not applicable for today. We are under the New Covenant. The King James version of the Bible is the only inspired version. If it was good enough for the Apostle Paul, then it's good enough for me. Did you see what Sister So-and-So was wearing last Sunday? I prayed for three hours last night, and thought you needed to know. It took us two hours to drive to church on Easter Sunday last year. I don't like the voice of that man. There is something that I don't like about him, but I just don't know what it is. Do you sense it too? I can teach better than that. That preacher doesn't preach enough about love. Why does he want me to get involved in church? After all that is what we pay him for. I can't go to that church because they put a demand on people. I'm not ready for that. I want to grow at my own pace. They should be glad I make it to church as often as I do."

Have you ever heard this voice? The voice of the religious spirit is found in dead and spiritually lifeless churches all over the world. But do not be deceived; religious spirits are not limited to any particular denomination. The religious spirit can be heard loud and clear even in the most on fire church you can think of.

One day I was invited out to lunch with some religious people. I had just left the church after a prayer gathering that they had not attended. We sat down at the dinner table and the man asked me to pray the blessing over the food. I prayed a short prayer and certainly not religious, mind you, something like, "Thank you for this food, Lord. Amen." I knew it was short, but there is nothing wrong with simple prayers of thanksgiving. Little did I know the Lord was getting ready to teach me another valuable lesson about the characteristics of the religious spirit.

To my surprise, this man was highly insulted by my brief prayer. He looked over at his wife and asked her to say the blessing the *right way*. Wow! I must admit it does bother me when praying over your lunch is the height of your spiritual communion with God. I believe in prayer, especially the quality of prayer, but long praying over meals is not, in most cases, the time for serious mountain moving, shaking, and quaking prayer.

If you ask religious people why they pray over their meals, they probably won't know. Most religious people pray from a spirit of tradition, rather than a heart that is compelled by a love for God's provision (1 Timothy 4:4-5). Others only pray over their meals because they are copying what they have seen others do or it's the behavior they believe is expected of them. You can expose a religious spirit almost every time by saying short prayers to bless the food at the dinner table and watching how they react.

You won't believe it, but I had another opportunity to have dinner with these same religious people. Well guess what happened? They asked me to pray again. I am sure they were wondering whether or not I could get it right this time. Well, the Spirit of God began to bubble up in me, and we began to have camp meeting right there at the dinner table. Praise the Lord! You should have seen their faces. Funny though, they stopped asking me to say grace. What happened?

TIT FOR TAT

Religious spirits seek to engage you in "tit for tat" as they offer legalistic rebuttles during conversations. There is no sense in going tit for tat with a religious spirit. We don't always have to defend God's Word. Be careful not to throw your pearls before swine (Matthew 7:6). Why continually open yourself up to religious abuse? This spirit will search for your weaknesses, not to help you to be an overcomer, but rather to use them as weapons to undermine your faith and walk with God. All this sounds so cruel, I know, but it happens all the time in churches across the globe. That's why this issue must be addressed. Religious people love to debate with you out of an argumentative heart.

Ask yourself these questions:

> Do certain people try to draw you into meaningless arguments and debate over the Word of God?

> Have you met the person that intentionally draws attention to themselves during prayer meetings?

Has anyone told you how long he or she prays in an attempt to prove his or her spirituality?

Are there people in your church who carry a self-righteous uppity religious attitude?

Has anyone ever accused you of being unloving when you were led by the Spirit of God to speak the truth in love?

If you answered yes to any of these questions, then you have no doubt encountered a religious spirit.

RELIGIOUS SCUFFLES

Putting those with religious spirits in positions of leadership is a death sentence in the ministry. Don't build a gallows for yourself by giving them the titles and positions they so covet. If you have already done so, then stay in the Spirit when dealing with them. Do not act out of your flesh, but at the same time, don't Mickey Mouse them and play religious mental games with them, either. The Word says, "Do not answer a fool in his folly" (Proverbs 26:4). Confront religious spirits head on when necessary. Remember, religious spirits do not take hints. Tell them outright what's the matter, in an attitude of love. Never speak out of the flesh, or anger, but rather out of a right spirit while communicating with Scriptural clarity and precision.

Pray for them and try to get them to see the weakness and the bondage of form, while leading them to the Lordship of Christ. Consider, however, that you can give a religious spirit a book, tape or CD that deals

Religious spirits will speak of controversial subjects, and to be sure, at inappropriate times.

with their problem specifically, and they will not see themselves in it. They will only see others.

If you approach them to bring loving, but strong correction, and they refuse to change, then cut them off. Don't use them in the church as workers or leaders. Never reward religious rebellion. Don't hesitate, because things will only get worse. Know the Word, and don't be afraid to open the Scriptures and discuss chapter and verse with them provided they are humble of heart and ready to receive.

By all means be sure to have somebody with you. Religious spirits hate witnesses during times of confrontation and correction. Why? Because it prevents them from twisting the truth. They cannot pervert what was said. They can't "smooth" over the correction and make light of it. The witnessed confrontation will either cause them to change or to decree and flee. Usually they'll flee because their motives are not pure.

SUMMARY
A FORM OF GODLINESS

Religious spirits sidetrack people with the deceptive illusion of form.

Religious spirits are into status, titles and position (Job 32:21-22).

What others think of a person with a religious spirit is more important to them than what God thinks.

Religious spirits are not teachable and seem to know it all.

Religious spirits are always critical of the way you do anything for God. No matter how you do it, they will always tell you that it could be done better.

Religious spirits spend a great deal of time talking about what great and magnificent things they are going to do for God, and then do nothing but criticize others.

Religious spirits will not get into agreement with, or get excited about the things of the Spirit. Instead they will buck, fight, argue, debate, and contend.

Religious spirits are typically gossips, always talking about the faults of others.

When exposed, religious spirits will accuse you of being unloving, hateful and non-Christ like.

Religious spirits view Jesus as a little lamb never offending, upsetting or contending with anyone (Luke 19:45).

In the next chapter, we will examine how these characteristics fit into a religious pattern.

CHAPTER 4

THE RELIGIOUS PATTERN

Religious spirits try to become the church's "religious advisors" while infecting you with a spirit of discouragement. Through the eyes of a religious spirit, the church is seen as a political ladder.

Now that we understand the characteristics of the religious spirit, we can explore its pattern. How does a religious spirit behave?

Religious spirits are usually very negative and full of religious excuses about why they are not doers of the Word. When you give them a Scripture to address a specific situation in their lives, they may say things like, "Well, you just really don't understand my situation," implying that no one else has ever been in the same terribly dark and awful position before.

The "letter of the law" (a legalistic view of the Word of God) can be their best friend as they seek to use the Word of God to bind people, rather than to liberate. They are powerful, nasty little spirits, and most dangerous to God's Kingdom. They covet the religious limelight and love to be the center of attention. Spiritual pride is a major pitfall in their lives. They think if God were going to do anything, He would surely use them and not you.

The "super spiritual" religious spirit will have fake moves of the Holy Spirit and operates in false spiritual government. You can tell when it's just their flesh manifesting because you feel sick to your stomach. If it's a devil, then the hair on the back of your neck may rise, or your blood pressure may go up. Let's take a look at some specific religious patterns.

IMPOSTERS

Religious spirits are hypocrites. Being hypocritical is both a characteristic and a pattern of this murderous spirit. They will tell you how wonderful you are to your face, but they will let you have it when you turn your back.

Religious spirits are masters at dodging pointed biblical answers to their faithless statements and questions. I have heard them many times respond to a Scriptural challenge saying, "That's not what I meant," when what they said is exactly what they meant. They just don't want you to zero in on their non-biblical foundational belief system. Religious spirits always try to get you to focus on someone or something else when they are being corrected because they

> **They will tell you how wonderful you are to your face, but they will let you have it when you turn your back.**

hate to be held accountable for their actions. Errors are never their fault. They think they never do anything wrong. Scripture says that God gives grace to the humble and resists the proud (James 4:6).

I have seen religious spirits attempt to explain away the power of God's Word, saying that it was for yesterday, but not for today. But the Word of the Lord says He does not change. He is the same yesterday, and today and forever (Hebrews 13:8).

POLITICS

In the last chapter we learned that one characteristic of the religious spirit is their hunt for position. That inclination fits into the religious pattern like a glove.

Religious spirits are the best players of religious politics, which is the quiet killer of both ministries and churches today. To advance their political agenda, religious spirits will join whatever opinion is religiously correct or fashionable at the time. I have even seen them join organizations, churches and small groups only to get close to people in leadership. Through the eyes of a religious spirit, everything is seen as a political ladder. Religious spirits will go out of their way to tell you how long they have been serving the Lord and believe that because of their "tenure," you should publicly recognize them and give them their due place of authority. They try to attach themselves to those who are actually called by God into the ministry for the purpose of control or selfish motivation. Watch out! They spend a lot of time thinking thoughts like, "What do I have to do, say, or act like in order to advance me, my, and mine to the top of the ladder in this church or ministry?" Unfortunately for them, they will discover that the top of the religious ladder is leaning against the wrong wall.

Religious spirits don't respect or submit to true spiritual authority. They give lip service to godly leadership, usurp authority and attempt to break ministry protocol whenever necessary to advance their selfish agendas. They appeal to and pet the flesh of others with flattery. They feel sorry for those who have been held accountable for some wrong action or who are being lovingly corrected by leadership. Their soulish emotions block true spiritual discernment in their own lives as they become religious stumbling stones in the lives of other people.

Ask yourself these questions:

Is there anyone in your life that just can't believe that the Holy Spirit would actually use you in ministry?

Do you know anyone who changes their opinion of Scripture based on what's politically correct or fashionable at the time?

Have you met the person who demands a leadership position or title based solely on their tenure rather than calling, availability to serve, or effectiveness in ministry?

Does anyone you know feel sorry for those who are being

held accountable for causing division in the church?

Have you ever been wrongly accused of being judgmental after expressing your beliefs?

Have you ever seen a person join a religious activity only to give them undue credibility?

If you answered yes to any of these questions, then you have observed the pattern of the religious spirit.

FAITH THIEVES

Religious spirits are the 21st century faith thieves. Doubt and unbelief are their closest friends. They will talk people right out of their blessings from the Lord, saying things like, "Well, we are not Jesus. You can't expect us to do the works He did. We just do the best we can." Those are unscriptural statements of false humility, and they stink of a religious spirit. They also say things like, "After all, we're only human." Religious spirits want to keep you from maturing in the Lord by undermining your faith in God and His Word.

Religious spirits also have a nasty habit of trying to ransack your joy. Have you ever shared a great hope of your heart with someone at church only to discover that his or her reaction was to put you down in an attempt to plunder your joy? What happened? Did you share your dream with the wrong person? Joy devouring is one of the sure signs of a religious spirit. When something wonderful happens to you, watch for those who rejoice with you. Look for the gleam in their eye. Listen for encouraging words of faith. Look for those who are laying hold of the vision. If you don't get a positive reaction, then beware of the religious spirit operating.

Ask yourself these questions:

> Has anyone attempted to discourage you and steal your God-given dreams?

> Has anyone provoked you to manifest emotionally in a negative way, then tried to use those negative emotions to chastise you?

> Has anyone ever discouraged you because they felt you were too emotional or fervent toward God?

Have you seen a lukewarm religious person hide behind their ability to quote Scripture as a facade to camouflage their apathetic spiritual condition?

If you answered yes to any of these questions, then the religious spirit has buffeted to you.

ANTI-CHRIST SPIRITS

The Holy Spirit within us will confirm and bear witness with the things of God, but because religious spirits are characteristically anti-Christ in nature (opposing the spiritual dynamic) they will not get into agreement with the things that are from the Spirit of God. That is why they are so disagreeable when you share what God has spoken to your heart.

Religious spirits will not get into agreement with, or get excited about the things of the Spirit. Instead they...

buck.

fight.

argue.

complain.

contend.

oppose.

discourage.

If they don't get enthused about the exciting things that God is doing in your life – watch out! You may be sharing your heart with a religious spirit.

PROVOKING

Religious spirits will speak of controversial subjects at inappropriate times. Watch out for that zinger in a meeting from this pious brother or sister.

Religious spirits can attack you with provoking words or use pietistic statements of discouragement, all the while expecting you to be completely emotionless to their attacks. It's all right for them to have a soulish emotion, but God forbid if you do.

Once a religious school teacher sent a very inflammatory letter to a mother about her daughter. The letter suggested that the daughter lacked "Christian character" and implied that it was because the mother herself did not have a high standard of character in accordance with his legalistic standards. Naturally, this letter upset the mother. The religious school teacher used this mother's emotional response to his self-righteousness as a weapon against her. When she met with him in a meeting he used the woman's provoked emotional response as a weapon to demean the woman and control the meeting. My heart goes out to single mothers who are doing the very

It's all right for them to have a soulish emotion, but God forbid if you do.

best that they can, yet are being chastised by religious spirits that criticize them to make themselves feel important.

We learned in the previous chapter that religious spirits speak out against displays of emotion. We also learned that these wicked spirits try to provoke you to anger like the religious school teacher who provoked the mother. Indeed, while religion hates emotion, they love to elicit the emotion of anger in an effort to murder your reputation. I have seen religious people use inflammatory words both verbally and in writing, *carefully chosen* to provoke a response or stir a negative emotion. If you become angry or just one bit emotional then they will use that provoked emotional display to condemn you. Religious spirits are masters at provoking you. This makes them feel good about themselves.

PASSION AND ANGER

Religious spirits also confuse passion with anger and come against any display of emotion as not being respectable or "decent and in order." They can provoke you to anger and then attack you for being upset or emotional at their assassination attempts.

Emotion itself is not evil.

God created us as expressive beings. He Himself is full of passion and emotion. Displays of emotion, even anger, are normal. I speak of the emotion of anger because it is the one emotion that religious legalists want to incite. Since they use it as a weapon against others let's review a few Scriptures about anger.

> Even Jesus Himself got angry at the religious scribes and Pharisees when they opposed His healing of the man on the Sabbath. Scripture declares, "And when he (Jesus) had looked round about them with anger (emotion), being grieved

(emotion) for the hardness of their hearts" (Mark 3:5).

The Word tells us, "Be ye angry, and sin not: let not the sun go down upon your wrath. Neither give place to the devil" (Ephesians 4:26-27).

The Word also says, "Not soon angry" (Titus 1:7), meaning not to be quick to anger. Again, this speaks of an uncontrollable anger.

Even the Apostles Paul and Peter had emotional displays recorded for all history to read (Galatians 2:12). Please understand, I am not giving any one a license to be angry, however, I am saying that the emotion of anger in and of itself should not be used to advance the efforts of a self-righteous religious spirit.

Jesus Himself displayed an emotion by cleaning out the temple with a whip (Matthew 21:12). Would we say that His show of emotion was below

the dignity permitted the office
of the King of kings and Lord
of lords? Did His driving out
the money changers violate
His witness?

So when someone with a religious spirit
attempts to provoke you to anger understand
they are doing it to make themselves look
good. But don't feel condemned if you showed
some passion or emotion. Be emotional just
don't sin.

BLACKMAIL

Religious spirits will try to blackmail you.
Sometimes religious people unplug or break
rank from their responsibilities in an effort
to get their own way. A person comes into
the church, seeks out positions and titles
and claims to love the church; yet refuses
to allow the Spirit of God and the Word of
God to change them and conform them into
the image of Christ. Instead of being a team
player, their pride wants them to be seen of
men and they want to be the next famous
Christian leader. They look at team ministry
as below them.

One time there was a musician on staff in
the church who thought he was God's calling
to the music ministry. He decided that he
wanted to be a pastor. Perhaps at some

future point in his life he may have been able to come into that. This man was very talented as a musician but was still a babe in Christ and was far from being ready to meet the challenges and pastoral responsibilities of a local church. When he asked one of the church's pastors if he thought he was ready to pastor a church, the pastor gracefully told him, "No." Of course, this musician didn't like that answer and missed several services in a row. Was this a manifestation of his pastoral maturity?

Those with religious spirits want you to chase after them.

The pastor made several unsuccessful attempts to get in touch with him. Then a couple weeks later the musician called to tell the pastor that he was coming back to the church the following weekend. The pastor told him that he would not be allowed on the platform to minister musically with the rest of the team until the matter was discussed and prayed through with repentance. That musician was never to be seen again. Do you think that he was really ready to be a pastor of a church? Later rumors and accusations were spread throughout the church by this musician accusing the pastor of being unloving.

Unfortunately many think that the ministry cannot function without them and they use it to control or to blackmail the leadership. These types of control and immature behavior are being exposed in our generation and are not being tolerated.

RELIGIOUS ABUSE

Religious spirits will abuse their leaders in the name of the Lord. They think that they are God-sent to be the pastor's personal religious assassins. These spirits try to get their pastors to become their religious attachés, in the name of being a servant (Acts 6:2, Ephesians 4:11-15). What they really want is for the pastor to be their personal servants, as they command and dispatch them to carry out their religiously correct agendas. How many pastors have felt guilty because of religious manipulation from this spirit?

A pastor told me of a lady who left his church when he was out of town with his family. The lady had a sick relative in her family who was dying in the hospital. The lady wanted the pastor to visit the relative in the hospital. When she could not get in touch with the pastor she was furious. The relative died and the lady left the church before the pastor returned. The pastor told me he made several attempts to contact the lady who refused to speak with him. The pastor told me that the relative that died had never been to the church in the 12 years that he was the leader. Nor did the lady ask one of the churches Elders to make the hospital visit. In her mind it was the pastor's job to visit the sick and no

Religious spirits will try to blackmail you.

one else's. Several questions arise, "Is this an unrealistic expectation of the pastor? Does the pastor have a responsibility to visit every sick relative of a church member even if they are not part of that church? Was it right to refuse to return the phone calls of the pastor?" Oftentimes religious spirits will defame their leaders when they don't perform according to their religious expectations. In this lady's mind the pastor was hired to perform such duties.

Religious spirits can have a spirit of confusion and instability around them. They may instill fear to obligate you to them. They may try to become the church's "religious advisors" while infecting you with discouragement. They typically draw their strength from demeaning and controlling others, and have a fear of not being in control of *others'* lives. Watch out, because the culmination of their activities will lead you into a spiritual wilderness.

> Religious spirits can even have an arrogant, "How dare you" attitude toward the anointing or any spiritual manifestation of the Holy Spirit.

They hold fast to the letter of the law, and are unforgiving forever. They can remember every uncomfortable thing that ever happened in their life. I have also noticed that religious spirits try to get you into agreement with their religious perspectives, and if you don't — look out! In many cases they know the truth, but are not lovers of the truth.

Religious spirits will call you things that you are not. God always delivers to you words of life, telling you who you are. When it comes to counseling for themselves, they want carnal sympathy, mushy love, flesh-petting, and not Holy Spirit, chapter and verse truth.

Ask yourself these questions:

> Have you ever seen a Christian worker in the church use their position to get their own way?

Have you ever met someone in church who felt the ministry couldn't survive without them and used that as a weapon against the leadership?

Have you ever seen a pastor who was abused by someone in the church?

Is there a particular religious tradition that is untouchable in your church?

Have you ever experienced the unforgiving attitude of the religious spirit?

TIME CONSUMERS

Another pattern of the religious spirit is time consuming. They come to your church for the first time on Sunday and immediately expect to book an appointment with the pastor. Religious spirits are controlling, time consumers and time thieves. I do my best not to engage myself in conversation with anyone right before I am about to preach. I have learned that the time right before the service is a strategic time for a religious spirit's provoking attack.

LUKEWARMNESS

Lukewarmness is the pathway to the religious spirit. Because of their backslidden spiritual condition, the religious spirit will attack and criticize your spiritual zeal and joy. Why? Because your presence brings conviction to their spiritual condition. The religious spirit will manifest a religious form and cling to traditions of men as a cloak to try and block others from discerning its true backslidden spiritual condition.

CLING TO TRADITION

Religious spirits always cling to form and tradition. How things were done in yesteryear is very important to them. They will be the first to stand against change, while they rally others to agree with their stance. They relax in their spiritual comfort zones with their arms crossed saying, "Bless me if you think you can, but I know you can't."

I was once on staff as an assistant pastor of a medium-sized church. The senior pastor went on vacation and asked me to fill in for him. Sunday came, and as I walked into the church, one of the deacons and his wife were starting to prepare the communion elements for a communion service. The pastor had not mentioned the communion service to me, so I prayed and felt that we should postpone it until the following Sunday when he was due back.

Well, you would have thought I had blasphemed the Holy Spirit. Many in the congregation became upset. After all, it was the first Sunday of the month. How dare the assistant pastor put off this sacred service until the following Sunday. I innocently stood

Is there a particular religious tradition that is untouchable in your church?

my ground against this religious attack as God taught me some valuable lessons. Religious spirits don't like flowing with the Spirit; they hate change. Watch out if you get between them and their religious tradition.

Remember that a seed bears fruit of its own kind. So it is with religious spirits. Left to propagate on their own, they will impose a death sentence on a Spirit-lifed church.

Someone once said, "The devil is married to a religious spirit and she gives birth to her children right in the church." The seducing spirit that will attempt to deceive the whole world will be a religious spirit. This alluring religious spirit will be one filled with religious activity and spiritualism, thus hampering the born again Christian's relationship with Jesus and bringing to a halt the journey of one destined to walk after the Spirit.

So how is it that one can start off in the Lord with zeal and fire and then end up bound in dead religious form? It is because of a series of choices that leads to religious bondage.

SUMMARY
THE RELIGIOUS PATTERN

The "super spiritual" religious spirit will propogate fake moves of the Holy Spirit and they operate in false spiritual government.

Religious spirits are hypocrites. They will tell you how great you are to your face but they will let you have it when you turn your back.

Through the eyes of a religious spirit, everything is seen as a political ladder.

Religious spirits don't respect or submit to true spiritual authority.

Religious spirits pet the flesh of others with smooth words and flattering sayings.

Religious spirits hate to be held accountable for their actions.

Religious spirits try to become the church's "religious advisors" while infecting you with a spirit of discouragement.

Religious spirits will spiritually abuse others.

Religious spirits always cling to form and tradition.

In the next chapter we will look at the significance of our will to pursue the Holy Spirit and a deeper walk with Jesus or take a detour and pursue the strange woman, the religious spirit personified. If we can see her in Scripture, then we can learn to avoid her at all cost.

CHAPTER 5

THE STRANGE
WOMAN

*The religious spirit is most dangerous with its words.
Religious spirits can be most polite and enticing and
engage you with flattering conversations. Beware,
there may be a serpent behind those ruby red lips!*

All of us are vulnerable to religious spirits, attitudes, or attacks of self-righteousness. We must choose, by our own wills, not to get involved. But how? Let's look in the seventh chapter of the Book of Proverbs for some Scriptural insight. For clarity let's replace "the strange woman" with the words "religious spirit."

In the first verse, we receive simple wisdom to help guard ourselves against religious spirits:

TREASURE THE WORD

"My son, keep my words, and
lay up my commandments with
thee" (Proverbs 7:1).

The word "keep" means to treasure. Do
you know how to place the Word in your
heart and treasure it? If you had five gold
bars, wouldn't you guard them from thieves
by putting them in a safe place? Well, if
the natural man would be careful about
things, then so should the spiritual man.
The Word of God and the commandments
of God should be guarded and treasured in
our hearts.

In the next two verses, Solomon expands
on his Spirit-led instruction in more detail:

"Keep my commandments,
and live; and my law as the
apple of thine eye. Bind them
upon thy fingers, write them
upon the tablet of thine heart"
(Proverbs 7:2-3).

You write the Word of God on the tablet of
your heart by meditation, musing, thinking
it over and over, by repeating it, etc. By doing
this, the Word gets written on your heart,
and when you need it the Holy Spirit will
bring it back to your memory.

Verse four urges the reader to embrace wisdom and understanding:

"Say unto wisdom, Thou art my sister; and call understanding thy kinswoman" (Proverbs 7:4).

A kinswoman is a most intimate friend. The word "intimacy" means, "come into me and see." From where does spiritual understanding come? It comes only from the Holy Spirit. We cannot understand God apart from the Spirit of God. He is the revealer of the Word. He is the one who gave Peter a different perception of Jesus. It is the Holy Spirit's job to reveal Jesus unto us. Therefore, we must regard Him as our most intimate friend.

We guard ourselves from religious spirits by treasuring the Word of God in our hearts and allowing the Holy Spirit to be our most intimate friend. Not the letter of the law of God, but the intimacy of the Spirit of God. Scripture says, "For the letter killeth, but the spirit giveth life" (2 Corinthians 3:6).

STRANGER TO GOD

In verse five, Solomon explains the result of the instruction in the first four verses of the proverb:

"That they may keep thee from the *strange woman*, from the stranger which flattereth with her words" (Proverbs 7:5 Italics added).

So we see that if you guard, as a treasure, the Word of God, meditate on the Word, make the Holy Spirit your most intimate friend, that will help guard you from the strange woman who is a type of the religious spirit.

Just like the religious spirit, one of the characteristics of this strange woman is "smooth words" spoken through flattering lips. She sounds good and, if need be, can get real spiritual. She has smooth sayings, but behind the facade of the strange woman is a religious spirit that is a stranger to the ways of God.

INEPT

In the next verses, we read how the strange woman (religious spirit) is looking for its victim. Religious spirits always try to set you up.

"For at the window of my house I looked through my casement, And beheld among the simple ones, I discerned among the youths, a young

man void of understanding"
(Proverbs 7:6-7).

The young man represents a Christian
who is not mature in Christ. He is immature,
a youth, and a spiritual babe. He has
some Word in him, he is progressing in
his perception of Jesus, but he is still a
youth. He is simpleminded and lacking in
spiritual discernment.

This young man was simpleminded
because the Holy Spirit was not yet his most
intimate friend. This was a simple person,
he lived and served God out of his mind. He
didn't seek God with the eyes of his heart.
Being spiritually half-witted, he sought and
served God through intellect and carnal
religious form.

Regardless of our age in Christ, all of us
have to guard ourselves from this strange
woman, the religious spirit. Her telltale
signs are smooth sayings as she dresses the
religious part looking for the carnal-minded.
We all must grow up spiritually. We cannot
stay spiritual babes. Age in the realm of the
Spirit is different than age in the natural.
You can be 60 years old physically and still
be a baby in spiritual things, or you can be
16 years old physically and be 60 in spiritual
things. We cannot serve God intellectually,
we must serve him out of the right spirit with
a heart full of faith.

Do you love your spouse intellectually; or do you love your spouse from your heart? When I see my daughters and grandchildren, my heart goes out to them, not my intellect. Religious spirits will latch on to those who know and serve God out of their mind only. Why? Because the carnal mind will hook up with the flesh and take one out into religious form and traditions.

AVOID HER HOUSE

In the next verse, we learn how one's will comes in to play in the destructive seductions of the religious spirit:

"Passing through the street near
her corner; and he went the way
to her house" (Proverbs 7:8)...

This simpleminded young man *willfully* went near the dwelling place of the strange woman, the religious spirit. He left the Word, guidance of the Holy Spirit as his most intimate friend, and began to serve God out of his mind and negelected his heart.

Lukewarmness will always point you in the direction of the religious spirit's house. This young man knew where the strange woman lived because he had been enticed and drawn by her smooth religious sayings.

She looked good and sounded good, surely to him this was right. This simpleminded fool made a willful choice to be led by his carnal soulish senses into religious form.

DEADLY RELIGIOUS GRIP

Verses nine and 10 illustrate religion's deadly grip:

> "In the twilight, in the evening, in the black and dark night: And, behold, there met him a woman with the attire of an harlot, and subtle of heart" (Proverbs 7:9-10).

The closer the young man got to her (religious) house, the more spiritual discernment he lost. Night began to fall on him, a denseness; he could no longer see as clearly as he could before. He was ready to fall into her deadly religious grip.

In verse 11, the young man finally meets her. She is sly and cunning with smooth words:

> "She is loud and stubborn; her feet abide not in her house" (Proverbs 7:11).

She is loud and turbulent in the soul. "Her feet abide not in her house," because she is never satisfied. She goes from church to church looking for the simpleminded to entice. She has a harlot's heart, the heart of a religious spirit. She will prostitute herself for self-gain and admiration of men. She loves positive public opinion and will compromise herself to gain it. Remember positive public opinion is very important to the religious spirit.

Verse 12 shows us how pervasive this nasty spirit is:

> "Now is she without, now in the streets, and lieth in wait at every corner" (Proverbs 7:12).

She is everywhere, in the marketplace, on the street corner, in the church, on the phone, in the Internet chat rooms; she is cunning and shrewd. She is looking for you. Watch out for her religious snares. Guard yourself. Maintain your spiritual hunger for more of God.

RELIGIOUS ACTIVITIES

In the next several verses, we read how the strange woman woos the simpleminded young man with religious activities:

"So she caught him, and kissed him, and with an impudent face said unto him, I have peace offerings with me; this day have I payed my vows. Therefore came I forth to meet thee, diligently to seek thy face, and I have found thee. I have decked my bed with coverings of tapestry, with carved works, with fine linen of Egypt. I have perfumed my bed with myrrh, aloes, and cinnamon. Come, let us take our fill of love until the morning: let us solace ourselves with loves. For the goodman is not at home, he is gone a long journey: He hath taken a bag of money with him, and will come home at the day appointed" (Proverbs 7:13-20).

She "paid her vows," and by doing so had appeased her conscience with dead works and religious activities. Now she is ready to do her own thing. How many people come to church on Sunday asking God for forgiveness and then live like the devil on Monday? This woman had no real change in her life. She had "decked her bed with coverings of tapestry and with carved works." All of this reveals the idolatry in her heart as she looks to create a religious facade. She has "perfumed her bed with myrrh, aloes and cinnamon." All this represents a false anointing and a religious covering on her life.

FAIR SPEECH

In the next verses we read about how the strange woman uses fair speech to entice:

> "With her much fair speech she caused him to yield, with the flattering of her lips she forced him. He goeth after her straightway, as an ox goeth to the slaughter, or as a fool to the correction of the stocks; Till a dart strike through his liver; as a bird hasteth to the snare, and knoweth not that it is for his life" (Proverbs 7:21-23).

The religious spirit is very dangerous with words. She can be most polite and enticing with flattering conversations. Beware, there is a serpent behind those ruby lips, ready with a dart to strike through the liver. The liver is the filter of the blood. The blood is the life force of the body.

THE WAY TO HELL

The final verses in the proverb reveal the motives of the strange woman, the religious spirit, and the fate of those that follow after her:

> "Hearken unto me now therefore, O ye children, and attend to the words of my mouth. Let not thine heart decline to her ways, go not astray in her paths. For she hath cast down many wounded: yea, many strong men have been slain by her. Her house is the way to hell, going down to the chambers of death" (Proverbs 7:24-27).

We must not let our hearts decline to her ways, nor stray in her paths. This is a free will choice that we can make. We must never serve God the *way* she does, through carnal and soulish form alone. We cannot learn her religious ways. We must stay away from her paths.

Religious paths are dead religious traditions that lead to her dwelling place. Not merely the newly saved are in potential danger. She can even destroy mature Christians if they go near her house. This is why the religious spirit needs to be unmasked. This beast sits in our churches unexposed and never addressed. She, the religious spirit, is the deadly killer of the lukewarm Christian.

Jesus said, "Hereafter I will not talk much with you: for the prince of this world cometh, and hath nothing in me" (John 14:30). If your heart and motivation is right, and you are not looking for titles or positions; if you are free from pride, manpleasing and the fear of men, then this spirit will not be able to influence you.

SUMMARY
THE STRANGE WOMAN

All of us are vulnerable to religious spirits, attitudes, or attacks of self-righteousness.

We must choose, by our own wills, not to travel the path of the religious spirit.

We can guard ourselves from religious spirits by treasuring the Word of God in our hearts and allowing the Holy Spirit to be our most intimate friend.

One of the characteristics of the strange woman is "smooth words" spoken through flattering lips.

Religious spirits will latch on to those that know and serve God out of their souls only.

Lukewarmness will always point you in the direction of the religious spirit's house.

The religious spirit is very dangerous with words. She can be most polite and enticing with flattering conversations.

The religious spirit is the deadly killer of the lukewarm Christian.

In the next chapter we will take a look at the Pharisees who are strong examples of those with religious spirits.

CHAPTER 6

THE PHARISEES

Pharisees, were teachers, interpreters and expounder's of the law of Moses, but they did not practice what they preached. Pharisees are strong examples of religious spirits.

When you think of religion, you no doubt think of those scribes and Pharisees that continually challenged Jesus and His ministry with their legalistic questions and objections. Pharisees are indeed the epitome of a religious spirit. Let's take a closer look at the scribes and Pharisees to better understand how Jesus perceived and dealt with the religious spirit.

The Pharisees were religious leaders of the time, but they were corrupted vessels. Jesus described them as white washed tombs full of dead men's bones. Jesus teaches us to make a distinction between God ordained, recognized positions of authority, such as Moses' seat (Greek *kathedra*, meaning seat of authority), and individuals that are occupying the seat at the time (Exodus 18:19-20). Why make such a distinction? Because...

> it is possible for a person who is called of God to set a poor example by his or her lifestyle.

Regardless, our responsibility remains as believers to respect God's seat of authority. We don't walk away from the truth of the Word of God and Jesus just because some may be corrupt.

> "Then spake Jesus to the multitude, and to his disciples, Saying, The scribes and the Pharisees sit in Moses' seat: All therefore whatsoever they bid you observe, that observe and do; but do not ye after their works: for they say, and do not" (Matthew 23:1-3).

In the Scripture above Jesus is addressing the *actions* of the Pharisees more than the teachings of the Pharisees. This is not to say that they did not teach some wrong doctrine and we will take a look at some such examples shortly. Obviously these Pharisees, who were teachers, interpreters and expounder's of the law of Moses who also advised the people how to handle particular situations, did not practice what they preached. Jesus said of this group, "they say and do not."

IMPERSONATORS

Those who say and do not are hypocrites. We've seen the characteristic and pattern of hypocrisy in the religious spirit. Now through further study of the Scriptures we will discover that hypocrisy is the dominate characteristic of the religious spirit as demonstrated by the scribes and Pharisees. The definition of a hypocrite, Greek *hupokrites*, is...

an actor.

a stage player.

a pretender.

a wearer of a mask.

one who puts up a facade.

one who hides behind a front.

one who offers lip service.

one who displays a quality he does not have.

an impersonator.

Religious hypocrites are those that know the Word of God, but refuse to do it. They are those that appear to be religious, yet do not serve God. They may have been very faithful at one time, but somewhere along the line they backslid and stopped progressing with God and living a righteous life in their hearts.

James told us that if you are a hearer of the Word of God only and not a doer of the Word of God then deception will come upon you (James 1:22).

This is one of the main reasons why there are so many religious people in churches today. They just simply will not live the life of faith by obeying the Word of God, therefore they end up becoming impostors (hupokrites). Are they still born again? Perhaps, but the Word tells us, "this people draw near me with their mouth, and with their lips do honor me, but have removed their heart far from me, and their fear toward me is taught by the precept of men" (Isaiah 29:13).

Deception leads to lukewarmness, another characteristic of the religious spirit. The Word declares, "So then because thou art lukewarm, and neither cold nor hot, I will spew thee out of my mouth" (Revelation 3:16).

The reason Jesus would rather have a person cold or hot instead of lukewarm is because of deception. A person who is cold knows that he is cold and a person who is hot knows that he is hot, but a person who is lukewarm thinks that everything is OK. That's religious deception. Then when one who is hotter comes into contact with the religious lukewarm person the religious spirit manifest.

Ask yourself these questions:

> Do you know religious people who tell you to do things that they don't do?
>
> Have you noticed the current religious fashions?
>
> Have you experienced the legalistic believer?
>
> Do you know someone who wears a religious mask?

HEAVY BURDENS

The Pharisees had hypocritical religious spirits that held people to standards that they themselves could not live up to. Scripture says of the religious,

> "For they bind heavy burdens and grievous to be borne, and lay them on men's shoulders; but they themselves will not move them with one of their fingers" (Matthew 23:4).

The ministry of the Holy Spirit and the Word of God is to liberate people. Jesus said, "Come unto me, all ye that labor and are heavy laden, and I will give you rest" (Matthew 11:28). But here again we find that the religious spirit would bind heavy burdens on people through a legalistic approach toward God rather than liberate them.

> To bind (Greek *desmeuo*) means to put one into chains.

One of the most visible marks of religious people is the opposition toward freedom of expression in worship. The Pharisees would bind people through...

legalism.

dead religious works.

false doctrines.

man's opinions.

traditions of men.

religious control.

Tradition says, "It has always been like this." Just because it has always been like this doesn't make it truth. The Word of God warns us of being entangled by the traditions of men in the following four Scriptures.

> 1.) "Let no man therefore judge you in meat, or in drink, or in respect of an holy day, or of the new moon, or of the sabbath days" (Colossians 2:16).

> 2.) "Now therefore, why do you test God by putting a yoke on the neck of the disciples which neither our fathers nor we were able to bear?" (Acts 15:10)

> 3.) "For it seemed good to the Holy Spirit, and to us, to lay upon you no greater burden

than these necessary things"
(Acts 15:28).

4.) "For not even those who are
circumcised keep the law, but they
desire to have you circumcised
that they may boast in your flesh"
(Galatians 6:13).

TO BE SEEN OF MEN

We see several examples in Scripture
of the Pharisees' attempts to be admired
of men. The religious spirit has impure
motives. Religious spirits love positions that
give them the appearance of being somebody
special. We should learn to know each other
by the spirit, Godly character and anointings
rather than the oftentimes deceitfulness of
titles. Scripture says,

> "But all their works they do for
> to be seen of men: they make
> broad their phylacteries, and
> enlarge the borders of their
> garments" (Matthew 23:5).

We learn that these Pharisees liked to
wear certain religious garments that set
them apart from the common dress of other
people. These religious garments drew
attention to their religious positions and,

of course, gave the illusion that these men were closer to God than others.

The Pharisees wore phylacteries. A phylactery was a strip of parchment inscribed with certain portions of the Pentateuch. It was rolled and placed in a small metal cylinder inside a square leather case. These cases were attached with straps to their foreheads and to the backs of their right hands. They saw wearing these phylacteries as a strictly literal interpretation of the Scripture,

> "And thou shalt bind them (the scripture) for a sign upon thine hand, and they shall be as frontlets between thine eyes. And thou shalt write them upon the posts of thy house, and on thy gates" (Deuteronomy 6:8-9).

Jesus said that they *made broad* their phylactery. These phylacteries were normally worn only during prayer, but the Pharisees appear to have worn them always and to have made them especially noticeable. They gave an air of being in strict obedience to the Word of God yet their hearts were not right with God. They wanted to be admired by the people.

The religious spirit is more concerned about outward things than inward things.

But our God looks upon the hearts of man as seen in the following Scriptures:

David said, "I have hidden thy word in my heart that I may not sin against thee" (Psalm 119:11).

"Oh let the wickedness of the wicked come to an end; but establish the just: for the righteous God trieth the hearts and reins" (Psalm 7:9).

"I the LORD search the heart, I try the reins, even to give every man according to his ways, and according to the fruit of his doings" (Jeremiah 17:10).

POSITION, TITLES, FLATTERY

We see in the following Scripture that the Pharisees also craved positions, titles and flattery. Jesus taught against coveting such things.

"And love the uppermost rooms at feasts, and the chief seats in the synagogues, And greetings in the markets, and to be called of men, Rabbi, Rabbi. But be not ye called Rabbi: for one is your Master, even Christ; and all ye are brethren. And call no man your father upon the earth: for one is your Father, which is in heaven. Neither be ye called masters: for one is your Master, even Christ. But he that is greatest among you shall be your servant. And whosoever shall exalt himself shall be abased; and he that shall humble himself shall be exalted" (Matthew 23:6-12).

It is not sitting in the chief seats of the churches or the best seats at the fellowship dinners that Jesus is condemning, but rather the *loving* of it. Again, we see the religious use of titles in this case by using the term Rabbi, Rabbi, meaning "teacher" or "master teacher."

Jesus is not telling us that we should not give honor where honor is due. He is not telling us to withhold respect from our leaders, but He is addressing the heart of those that are religious, those that thrive on titles and those that make a distinction that separates them from the common folk.

Religion exalts itself above others and looks down on people.

Jesus teaches that those that do things to be admired of men already have their reward. Jesus teaches humility. Jesus teaches that we should not elevate one person above another. And Jesus teaches that we are to glorify God. The following Scriptures teach us how to guard our hearts:

"Do not exalt yourself in the presence of the king, And do not stand in the place of the great; For it is better that he say to you, "Come up here," Than that you should be put lower in the presence of the prince, Whom your eyes have seen" (Proverbs 25:6-7).

"Be kindly affectioned one to another with brotherly love; in honor preferring one another" (Romans 12:10).

"My brethren, have not the faith of our Lord Jesus Christ, the Lord of glory, with respect of persons. For if there come unto your assembly a man with a gold ring, in goodly apparel, and there come in also a poor man in vile raiment; And ye have respect to him that weareth the gay clothing, and say unto him, Sit thou here in a good place; and say to the poor, Stand thou there, or sit here under my footstool: Are ye not then partial in yourselves, and are become judges of evil thoughts?" (James 2:1-4)

"But as we were allowed of God to be put in trust with the gospel, even so we speak; not as pleasing men, but God, which trieth our hearts. For neither at any time used we flattering words, as ye know, nor a cloak of covetousness; God is witness: Nor of men sought we glory, neither of you, nor yet of others, when we might have been burdensome, as the apostles of Christ" (1 Thessalonians 2:4-6).

A PHARISEE MARRIAGE

Let's look at the destructiveness of the religious spirit in a marriage.

Once a lady asked her pastor to provide marriage counseling to her and her husband.

She was deeply concerned about the spiritual condition of her husband and indicated it was severally affecting their marriage.

During several meetings the wife would direct focus on her husband's faults and his lack of spiritual leadership in the home. She continually mentioned that he would not pray with her. As the counseling sessions continued, however, the meetings took a different turn.

After wading through all the accusations it became clear that not all of the marriage difficulties were the husband's fault. In fact, the husband said that his wife wanted him to get up each morning and pray with her and have Bible study each morning at 6:00 a.m. He refused because of his work schedule and agreed to pray with her at 7:00 a.m. instead. She then refused and challenged his commitment level to the Lord. The husband told the pastor that his wife would engage him each morning with condescending remarks challenging his spiritual condition. Repeatedly she emphasized the number of years that she was born again compared to him, the amount of Scripture she knew compared to him and the amount of time she prayed compared to him.

It came up also that the wife had withheld sexual relations from her husband for over six months that produced an intense anxiety in her husband. But when this was brought up during the counseling session she got up from the table refusing to discuss it, subsequently stopping any further counseling sessions.

After she refused any further meetings she left the church making several phone calls to members saying how unloving and non-understanding the pastor was.

It became apparent that the woman was intentionally withholding intimacy from her husband in an effort to get him to sin. She even began to invite an attractive divorced woman to her home whom she suspected her husband might be attracted to. Later the pastor found out that she had hoped that her husband would commit adultery with this other woman. This unfaithfulness, in her mind, would release her Scripturally from the marriage and she would remain in good standing with God, her religious friends and be free to seek out another man. Religion is an evil spirit that will go to any length to destroy people's lives.

The woman's husband, however, chose to remain faithful to his wife. He loved her and wanted to do every thing possible to work things out. He tried to take his place as the spiritual leader in his home but she continued to find fault with him and added many insulting religious criticisms. In reality every time the husband attempted to enter his position as the spiritual leader of the home she refused to submit to his leadership. The couple is now divorced.

Here again we see the work of a religious spirit. Notice the legalism, faultfinding, criticism, provoking, hypocrisy, rebellion and elaborate scheming of this woman. Anyone who would try to get their spouse to commit adultery to give them a Scriptural way out of a marriage covenant has been overcome by a religious spirit.

SUMMARY
THE PHARISEES

Pharisees, were teachers, interpreters and expounder's of the law of Moses, but they did not practice what they preached.

Pharisees are strong examples of religious spirits.

Those who say and do not are hypocrites.

Religious hypocrites are those that know the Word of God, but refuse to do it.

A person who is spiritually cold knows that he is cold and a person who is hot knows that he is hot, but a person who is lukewarm thinks that everything is OK.

To bind (Greek *desmeuo*) means to put one into chains.

In the next chapter we look more deeply into Jesus responses to the Pharisees' religious spirit – the eight woes of Jesus.

CHAPTER 7

THE EIGHT
WOES OF JESUS

Jesus is a loving Shepherd, but He is also as bold
as a lion when dealing with religious spirits. Let's
take a look at some of the most severe words that
Jesus ever spoke – the eight woes – and to whom He
spoke them.

No teaching on the religious spirit
would be complete without review-
ing the eight woes of Jesus. His
extreme sorrow and deep anguish is revealed
to us as He addresses the religious scribes
and Pharisees. These scribes and Pharisees
are types of modern-day carnal religious
people that possess a religious spirit. Many
people fail to recognize that the Word of God
exposes *the wolves* (Acts 20:29, 30), *the*
dogs (Philippians 3:2), *the deceitful workers*
(2 Corinthians 11:13) and, in the Gospel

according to St. Matthew, the religious spirits. The woes themselves give us clear insight into the major characteristics of the religious spirit. The eight woes teach us that religious spirits...

1. Shut up the Kingdom of heaven.

2. Put on a show.

3. Raise false sons.

4. Are blind guides and fools.

5. Are legalistic hypocrites.

6. Are full of extortion and excess.

7. Are pretty tombs.

8. Possess a murdering spirit.

As we undergo a deep examination of the eight woes of Jesus we will learn more about the woeful traits of the religious leaders that opposed the Gospel. We will also see the gentle Jesus using the most severe language in Scripture as He addresses the religious spirit.

The word "woe" is the Greek word *ouai,* which is a deep felt expression of grief. The word is also used to refer to those religious spirits that cause...

great sorrow.

grief.

misery.

affliction.

trouble.

frustration.

THE FIRST WOE

SHUT UP THE
KINGDOM OF HEAVEN

In the first woe Jesus teaches us that religious spirits are carnal hypocrites that stand as legalistic guards against the deep spiritual and meaningful things of God. They won't enter in themselves, nor will they permit you to enter in.

"But woe unto you, scribes and Pharisees, hypocrites! for you shut up the kingdom of heaven against men: for you neither go in yourselves, neither suffer ye them that are entering to go in" (Matthew 23:13).

Shutting up the Kingdom of heaven against men is a very common activity of religious people that neither advance nor increase in the things of God or allow anyone else to, either. They stand as demonic guards and buffet the things of the Spirit of God – all in the name of religious duty. The following Scriptures are examples of religious spirits that shut up the Kingdom of heaven.

"Woe unto you, lawyers! for ye have taken away the key of knowledge: ye entered not in yourselves, and them that were entering in ye hindered" (Luke 11:52).

"But that it spread no further among the people, let us straitly threaten them, that they speak henceforth to no man in this name. And they called them, and commanded them not to speak at all nor teach in the name of Jesus" (Acts 4:17-18).

"Saying, Did not we straitly command you that ye should not teach in this name? and, behold, ye have filled Jerusalem with your doctrine, and intend to bring this man's blood upon us. Then Peter and the other apostles answered and said, We ought to obey God rather than men" (Acts 5:28-29).

Notice that these religious spirits had two distinctly evil traits: hindering and threatening. First, by hindering those who were entering into the substance of Spirit-life living and a deeper, more intimate relationship with the Lord, the religious spirits took away the key of knowledge. Without knowledge and an accurate perception of Jesus we can never mature spiritually or renew our minds (Romans 12:1-3). If we don't think right, then we can't believe right and if we don't believe right, then faith is made void through ignorance. Secondly, we see that the religious spirits threatened those who were pursuing more than carnal religious form and lifeless traditions of men.

Ask yourself these questions:

Have you ever felt threatened or strongly opposed for your

spiritual intimacy with the Lord Jesus Christ?

Has anyone ever blocked Scriptural truth from being taught to you?

Have you ever had to determine in your heart that you were just going to put God first even though you were being opposed in doing so?

Has anyone ever made fun of your spirituality or your relationship with Jesus?

If you answered yes to any of these questions, then a religious spirit may have hindered you.

Still others shut up the Kingdom of heaven by opposing personal prophecy, fervent prayer, speaking in tongues, praying for the sick, singing *that* song, going to *that* church, and so on.

Keep in mind that sometimes shutting up the Kingdom of heaven can be less obvious. It can be as subtle as not being supportive of your church's leadership. So rather than getting behind the vision and helping, for example, the religious spirit refuses to cooperate. The religious spirit prefers to buck, argue, complain, debate, and otherwise avoid helping the cause, thus frustrating the plans of God. Moreover, through apathy the religious spirit hinders God's plan for the church. All of us must beware of the religious spirit who shuts up the Kingdom of heaven.

THE SECOND WOE

RELIGIOUS SPIRITS
PUT ON A SHOW

In the second woe of Jesus we discover that religious spirits will put on a show. In the Scripture below "for a pretence" could be translated "to put on a show."

> "Woe unto you, scribes and Pharisees, hypocrites! for you devour widows' houses, and for a *pretence* make long prayer: therefore ye shall receive the greater damnation" (Matthew 23:14, Italics added).

Once I attended a church service at which a preacher was about to minister to those in attendance. Throughout the day he dropped names of well-known Gospel leaders. The inference was that he had a personal relationship with each of them. Of course, it was obvious that he was just trying to make himself look important. He even boasted about having breakfast with the City Mayor. Of course, he failed to mention that the Mayor's Breakfast was open to anyone and many other pastors and leaders were also present. He gave the false impression that he was the only pastor having breakfast with the Mayor.

They won't enter in themselves, nor will they permit you to enter in.

In his conversations he also mentioned that he wore certain clothes because one of these well-known Gospel leaders had once told him it was important to dress that way in order to be taken seriously. His clothes were dazzling and chic and he pastored a church that looked like a studio set straight from a Christian TV program. Everything was polished, shined and fashioned just so. Not a single detail was left undone. As I stood watching I couldn't help but think the show was about to begin. As my British friends might say, we were about to get the Full Monty. This pretentious pastor preached and wowed the crowd, ending with a spiritual sounding prophecy full of false decrees. Then, after a full spin and a half, he fell on the floor supposedly so overwhelmed by the power of God he could stand no more – the show was over.

Sadly, this poor fellow didn't impress anyone. Those mature believers saw right through his selfish and soulish *pretense* and never came back to the show for Act 2. Scripture says,

> "Be not rash with thy mouth, and let not thine heart be hasty to utter any thing before God: for God is in heaven, and thou upon earth: therefore let thy words be few" (Ecclesiastes 5:2).

I heard this prayer from a person once when leaders from several churches got together to petition the Lord for revival in the city. "Oh Lord, we know that the Christian television station wants to have me on their program and that the Christian magazine wants to interview me. Thank you for all the open doors, but I just don't want to miss you God. I just want to remain humble in your sight. Thank you Lord that Pastor Famous Christian wants to preach in my church, but I just don't want to miss your timing. Oh Lord, you are the one who gives me favor with my city's leaders and the President's

prayer initiative at the White House, etc."
All I can say is: Yuck! This is the type of
a showy prayer with false humility that
intends to mislead and is used to impress
those who are listening – that's a pretense.
Then, of course, there is the person that
wants to make glitzy prayers to impress
people over meals and prays for everything
and everybody – then forgets to give thanks
to God for the food. Jesus is not pleased with
the polished showmanship of the religious
deceiver whose motive is the show.

Ask yourself these questions:

> Have you ever experienced a
> religious show that was nothing
> more than a demonstration of a
> false anointing?

> Do you know a person who prays
> for everything and everybody
> – but only at meal times?

> Have you heard the prayer that
> sounds like a self-promotional
> radio advertisement?

> What about the person that
> turns a testimony time into a
> preaching opportunity?

Have you ever heard a prayer
that was full of false humility?

If you answered yes to any of these
questions, then you have likely witnessed
the pretence of the religious spirit.

THE THIRD WOE

FALSE SONS

In the third woe Jesus declares that the
Pharisees are hypocrites that do everything
possible to raise up religious sons just as
legalistic as themselves.

> "Woe unto you, scribes and
> Pharisees, hypocrites! for you
> compass sea and land to make
> one proselyte, and when he is
> made, ye make him twofold
> more the child of hell than
> yourselves" (Matthew 23:15).

The whole world is waiting for the
manifestation of the sons of God (Romans
8:19). People with religious spirits, however,
are not interested in the development of
true sons of God. They work on duplicating
others after their own religious images rather
than sons of God who are conformed into

His image. The religious spirit will scour the church looking for that perfect candidate for its religious indoctrination program.

I remember a very religious woman that targeted a couple that had been terribly hurt and rejected. She counseled and prayed for them at length, creating an unhealthy soul tie that bound them to her and pulled them out of their local church. This woman made herself out to be more spiritual and understanding of this couple's needs than those in leadership at their church. All of this was an effort to prove her superior qualifications and spirituality. These actions elevated her para-church (outside the local church) ministry above the importance of the local church. This is a strategy of the religious spirit – to isolate its prey from true spiritual covering with false mentoring that creates unhealthy soul ties. The ultimate goal, of course, is to create false sons.

Ask yourself these questions:

> Has anyone tried to use the Word of God to control you?

> Has anyone ever tried to plug you into themselves rather than the local church?

Have you ever experienced the formation of an unhealthy soul tie with a religious person?

Do you know someone who knows lots of Scripture but doesn't grasp the spiritual meaning of those Scriptures?

Have you met religious people that make vows and commitments but don't keep their word?

Have you met the person that likes the religious debate and splitting of doctrinal hairs?

If you answered yes to any of these questions, then a religious spirit has tried to manipulate you.

THE FOURTH WOE

BLIND GUIDES AND FOOLS

In woe four Jesus zeros in on the Pharisees' inability to lead the righteous. He labels them as blind guides and fools that have no spiritual understanding of the Word of God. A religious spirit can never lead people into a greater walk with Jesus because one cannot take someone to a place that one has not already been.

Religious spirits may know the current religious buzzwords and Christian lingo, but they are faultfinders that put down those with true spiritual discernment while they live a life directed by carnal religion. In woe four Jesus says,

> "Woe unto you, ye *blind guides,* which say, Whosoever shall swear by the temple, it is nothing; but whosoever shall swear by the gold of the temple, he is a debtor! Ye *fools* and blind: for whether is greater, the gold, or the temple that sanctifieth the gold? And, Whosoever shall swear by the altar, it is nothing; but whosoever sweareth by the gift that is upon it, he is guilty. Ye fools and blind: for whether is greater, the gift, or the altar that sanctifieth the gift? Whoso therefore shall swear by the altar, sweareth by it, and by all things thereon. And whoso shall swear by the temple, sweareth by it, and by him that dwelleth therein. And he that shall swear by heaven, sweareth by

the throne of God, and by him
that sitteth thereon" (Matthew
23:16-22, Italics added).

The Pharisees were teaching that if you
swore by the temple or by the altar, then
you were not bound to keep your word.
But if you swore by the *gold* of the temple
or by the *gift* on the altar, then your word
was binding.

Amazing how the love of money corrupted
their decisions. They were legalistically
splitting hairs and they were placing the
emphasis on material things rather than
upon the spiritual purpose for which they
were to be used. Religious spirits are blind
guides and fools.

THE FIFTH WOE

LEGALISTIC HYPOCRITES

In woe five Jesus once again exposes
the true nature of a religious spirit –
a hypocrite.

"Woe unto you, scribes and
Pharisees, hypocrites! for ye
pay tithe of mint and anise and
cummin, and have omitted the
weightier matters of the law,

> judgment, mercy, and faith:
> these ought ye to have done,
> and not to leave the other
> undone. Ye blind guides, which
> strain at a gnat, and swallow a
> camel" (Matthew 23:23-24).

This fifth woe pictures the Pharisees again with their emphasis on externals. This is a picture of the average church today that is busy making the outside of the cup look clean by religious works but never deals with matters of the heart. They go through all the ceremonies, have the best sound equipment, chairs, buildings, etc. But all of the external ceremonies cannot clean up the corruption of the inner man. The Pharisees substituted...

ritual for reality.

formality for faith.

liturgy and form for true worship.

The Pharisees would pull their ox out of a ditch on the Sabbath (Luke 14:5), but were furious when someone was healed (Luke 13:16) on the Sabbath. They cared more about the religious keeping of rules and traditions more than they did about people.

Once I met a man who seemed to be a devout Christian. After getting to know him better I discovered that he was so legalistic that he would not let his children view even a Disney movie. This man's wife frequently called the ministry for help after he beat her. See the hypocrisy? Again Scripture says,

> "Ye blind guides, which strain
> at a gnat, and swallow a camel"
> (Matthew 23:24).

"Strain at a gnat" is more accurately translated "strain out a gnat." The Jews strained wine before drinking it so as to avoid touching or swallowing anything unclean. So we can see that these religious leaders were so utterly legalistic that they would "strain out a gnat" before they drank, but would "swallow a camel." Blinded leaders, indeed. Just like the man who refused to allow his children to view a Disney movie but finds it OK to beat his wife.

FOUR EXAMPLES OF LEGALISM

1.) Before Judas hanged himself he threw the silver pieces paid to him for betraying Jesus into the temple. The chief priests decided it was not legal to put it into the treasury because it was blood money (Matthew 27:6). So we see that these legalistic religious spirits could pay for the murder with the money but not take the money back.

2.)   When Jesus was taken from Caiaphas to the building where the Roman governor stayed, the crowd waited outside and cried out against Jesus. But they would not go inside the building because they might defile themselves and become unclean and be barred from eating the Passover meal (John 18:28). It was OK to cry out, "Crucify him" as long as they didn't enter the building.

3.)   The Pharisees and teachers of the law asked Jesus, "Why do thy disciples transgress the tradition of the elders? for they wash not their hands when they eat bread." Jesus' reply was in the form of a question, "Why do ye also transgress the commandment of God by your tradition?" (Matthew 15:2-3). Again we see the outward focus by the religious spirit.

4.)   After Jesus went to the Father, some believers that belonged to the party of the Pharisees continued to try to put their legalistic demands on Christians, saying, "It is necessary to circumcise [the Gentile converts] and to charge them to obey the Law of Moses" (Acts 15:5 AMP).

LEGALISM TODAY

Religious spirits are legalistic and typically use the letter of the law as a weapon to bind one's liberty. The following is an example in which the letter of the law clearly violates the spirit of the law.

According to a report in the *Readers Digest,* 12-year-old Christina Roads, an honor student at Maryland Middle School, was an asthmatic. While riding the school bus, Christina saw fellow student Brandy Dryer, also an asthmatic, begin to gasp for breath. Christina, fearing for Brandy's

Sadly, this poor fellow didn't impress anyone.

life, gave Brandy her prescription inhaler. Brandy's grateful mother believed Christina's actions saved Brandy's life.

School officials, however, weren't pleased. The school's "Zero Tolerance" drug policy prohibits students from sharing medicine. And what is saving a life compared to violating school policy? Because the incident took place on school property (a school bus) officials filed a report criticizing Christina for violating school drug regulations. The report will remain on file as long as she attends the school.

THE SIXTH WOE

FULL OF
EXTORTION AND EXCESS

In woe six Jesus exposes the religious sin of extortion and excess.

> "Woe unto you, scribes and Pharisees, hypocrites! for ye make clean the outside of the cup and of the platter, but within they are *full of extortion and excess*. Thou blind Pharisee, cleanse first that which is within the cup and platter, that the outside of them may be clean also" (Matthew 23:25-26, Italics added).

The cup represents one's life. Don't misunderstand Jesus. He is not saying that the outside of the cup should not be clean. However, the emphasis should never be on the outside of the cup *only* while we neglect the inside (the heart). Jesus uses some very strong words when He says the Pharisees were full of extortion. Extortion is, the act of plundering, robbery and stealing.

Extortion is a predetermined plan of action with the intent to steal from someone. Jesus said the Pharisees were so full of excess that they had lost the ability to control their lust for more. Today we have modern religious merchandisers who steal from the people of God so they can lavish themselves with excess.

Ask yourself these questions:

Have you ever been the victim of the letter of the law?

Have you ever heard an unsaved man command his wife to submit to his every whim because he is the head of the house and the Bible teaches that wives should submit to their husbands?

Have you ever been robbed from or deceived by someone you thought was an honest Christian?

Has anyone ever manipulated you with Scripture in an effort to steal your money?

Have you ever attended a church that was beautiful on the outside but inside there was no spiritual life?

If you answered yes to any of these questions, then you have seen the operations of the religious spirit.

THE SEVENTH WOE

A PRETTY TOMB

In woe seven we learn that the religious spirit is nothing more than a pretty tomb.

> "Woe unto you, scribes and Pharisees, hypocrites! for ye are like unto whited sepulchers, which indeed appear beautiful outward, but are within full of dead men's bones, and of all uncleanness. Even so ye also outwardly appear righteous unto men, but within ye are full of hypocrisy and iniquity" (Matthew 23:27-28).

It was commonly believed that if anyone could get into heaven, if anyone were righteous, surely it would have to be the Pharisees. Why? Because people were looking at their supposed pious and religious works. But Jesus called them dead, full of hypocrisy and iniquity. He then went on to say that they were full of uncleanness, which means they were full of impure motives and lust. One can only imagine the impact of such statements that Jesus made. No wonder they wanted to kill him.

Have you ever been to a graveyard and seen all the different types of grave markers? Some are covered with beautiful carved granite with sentimental remarks, along with the date of birth and death of the person. Then there are other graves that are enclosed by marble structures with wrought iron entrance gates. These tombs are works of art towering above all the other graves in the cemetery. They might be visually impressive, but at the end of the day, like every other grave, they simply house the departed.

A "whited sepulcher" is just a pretty tomb. It looks nice but it is nothing more than a house for the dead. Jesus likened the whited sepulcher to the religious spirit that outwardly appears righteous but inside is full of hypocrisy, iniquity and spiritual death. Today we see beautiful multi-million dollar buildings, but, sad to say, some are full of dead men's bones and religious spirits.

Ask yourself these questions:

> Have you met the person that respects the great revivalist of history but disrespects those

who have the same revivalist spirit today?

Do you know anyone who went off to Bible School full of zeal and returned backslidden, legalistic and carnal?

Do you know people who have embraced Christian philosophy but not Jesus, the founder of Christianity?

If you answered yes to any of these questions, then you have seen the impact of the religious spirit.

THE EIGHTH WOE

A MURDERING SPIRIT

Finally, woe number eight reveals to us the shocking murderous heart of a religious spirit. Let's read Jesus' final and most stern declaration.

> "Woe unto you, scribes and Pharisees, hypocrites! because ye build the tombs of the prophets, and garnish the sepulchers of the righteous,

And say, If we had been in the days of our fathers, we would not have been partakers with them in the blood of the prophets. Wherefore ye be witnesses unto yourselves, that ye are the children of them which killed the prophets. Fill ye up then the measure of your fathers. Ye serpents, ye generation of vipers, how can ye escape the damnation of hell? Wherefore, behold, I send unto you prophets, and wise men, and scribes: and some of them ye shall kill and crucify; and some of them shall ye scourge in your synagogues, and persecute them from city to city" (Matthew 23:29-34).

Jesus taught us there is a murderous motive in the heart of the religious spirit. The religious talk about how they love our forefathers – great men of God, preachers, evangelists, and missionaries that were denounced and ridiculed while they were alive, but today are often honored – yet these same religious spirits are the very hindrances to contemporary revival. These same religious leaders that were honoring the prophets of the past were soon to crucify the very Son of God who was speaking to them.

I have known young men and women with a zeal and love for Jesus that attended Bible School only to return totally drained of their love for God. Their spiritual fervency was murdered. What happened? Could it be that they were exposed to the religious spirit that honors the prophets of old but kills the prophets of

Have you heard the prayer that sounds like a self-promotional radio advertisement?

today? I am all for Christian education as long as it is not void of Holy Spirit impartation.

Once I met an unsaved woman who enrolled her child in a Christian academy because she wanted her child to have good morals. She never considered the importance of her child's salvation. Serving Jesus is more than being indoctrinated in Christian philosophy or religions theology; it is an active heart felt love for our Savior and King.

Jesus ends this woe by calling the religious spirits "serpents" and "vipers." The strongest of words toward the religious from the King of kings and Lord of lords. Let's look at some other examples of the murdering religious spirit.

> The day that Stephen was stoned to death, the young Saul whose name would soon be changed to the Apostle Paul, stood by and guarded the garments of those that murdered an innocent man (Acts 7).

> Cain murdered his brother Abel because he was jealous and angry with God because Abel's offering to God was accepted and his wasn't (Genesis 4).

The religious spirit is not limited to Christianity. In the city of Mecca, 15 young girls died in a raging fire as Saudi Arabia's religious police, known as the "mutaween," beat them back with rods and stopped them from leaving a school building because they were not wearing headscarves and abayas (black robes), which are required by the kingdom's strict interpretation of Islam.

The father of one of the dead girls said that the school watchman refused to open the gates to let the girls out. To these religious zealots it was better for the children to die than to be rescued if they weren't wearing the legal attire. Saudi's religious police also roam the streets to enforce dress codes and ensure that prayers are performed on time. Women walking alone are interrogated; some are even beaten to teach them a lesson before being released.

I still remember what Muslim leader Osama bin Laden said after the attacks of September 11th, 2001 during which Muslim extremists hijacked three airplanes, two that

The religious spirit is a murdering spirit.

plowed into the Twin Towers in New York City, killing thousands of innocent people. He said, "This is a war between the believer and the unbeliever." Those were profound words spoken by someone with a murderous religious spirit. From those words, and the attacks themselves, the world saw firsthand the manifestation of the murdering spirit of religion. This same woe of Jesus applies to all religions with murderous motives, "Ye serpents, ye generation of vipers, how can ye escape the damnation of hell?" (Matthew 23:33)

The eight woes of Jesus reveal His heart toward those with religious spirits. Scripture boldly admonishes us, "Having a form of godliness, but denying the power thereof:

from such turn away" (2 Timothy 3:5). These woes all have one thing in common: the total distain of the Lord Jesus Christ and His deepfelt expression of grief.

SUMMARY
THE EIGHT WOES OF JESUS

The Word of God exposes the wolves (Acts 20:29, 30), the dogs (Philippians 3:2), the deceitful workers (2 Corinthians 11:13) and the religious spirits (2 Timothy 3:5).

Shutting up the Kingdom of heaven against men is a very common activity of religious people that do not advance or increase in the things of God or allow anyone else to.

For pretence means to put on a show.
The religious put a strong emphasis on external perception.

Religious spirits are legalistic and typically use the letter of the law as a weapon to bind one's liberty.

Extortion is a predetermined plan of action with the intent to steal from someone.

A "whited sepulcher" is just a pretty tomb.

The religious raise up legalistic sons like themselves.

The spirit of religion is a murdering spirit.

In the final chapter let's learn more about protecting ourselves from the evil of the religious spirit.

CHAPTER 8

PROTECTION
FROM RELIGION

Maintaining a fervent prayer life is absolutely critical to advancing in your walk with Jesus. If you're lacking in this area, then you're already in spiritual trouble. Lukewarmness is the number one entryway for the religious spirit.

The religious spirit targets the backslidden. All of us must guard our spiritual hunger and zeal for the Lord Jesus Christ. Scripture says that we must work out our own salvation with fear and trembling (Philippians 2:12). We must examine our hearts which can only be between us and the Lord Himself. We must get back to the place spiritually that we once were. It's OK to repent of apathy and lukewarmness and start over again. Scripture says, "If we confess our sins He is faithful and just to forgive us our sins and to cleanse us from all unrighteousness" (1 John 1:9).

It's also important to examine our commitment and pursuit level. Ask yourself these questions:

> Are you spiritually cold, hot, apathetic or lukewarm?

> Have you slipped back from that place in God that you once were?

These are all roads that point toward the religious spirits house.

> What about your prayer life?
> Are you growing in that area?

Developing a private and corporate prayer life is vital for every believer.

> Are you plugged into a great church? Or a lifeless church?

Being part of the right local church is extremely important to you. Emotional soulties to dead churches will rob from you every time. Find a great Spirit-lifed church and get involved. Scripture says that we must be "planted" if we are to "flourish" (Psalm 92:13).

When religion attacks us it also elevates spiritual pride. Pride says that you are better than others. This releases self-righteousness and an inability to receive correction. We must all remain humble, be a doer of the Word, watch our associations, avoid carnality, legalism and remain teachable.

The following is a list of Scriptures that will help shield us from the religious spirit. Meditating on these Scriptures will lead you toward freedom from this nasty spirit and protect you from its influence.

SUBMISSION

"Obey them that have the rule over you, and submit yourselves: for they watch for your souls, as they that must give account, that they may do it with joy, and not with grief: for that is unprofitable for you" (Hebrews 13:17).

HUMILITY

"Likewise, ye younger, submit yourselves unto the elder. Yea, all of you be subject one to another, and be clothed with humility: for God resisteth the proud, and giveth grace to the humble" (1 Peter 5:5).

CORRECTION

"All scripture is given by inspiration of God, and is profitable for doctrine, for reproof, for correction, for instruction in righteousness" (2 Timothy 3:16).

TEACHABLE

"Study to show thyself approved unto God, a workman that needeth not to be ashamed, rightly dividing the word of truth" (2 Timothy 2:15).

BEWARE OF ADMIRATION

"But Peter and John answered and said unto them, Whether it be right in the sight of God to hearken unto you more than unto God, judge ye" (Acts 4:19).

We are all susceptible to this self-righteous religious spirit. No one is immune.

There are however, safeguards to keep us from its deceptive grip. Let's continue.

MAINTAIN YOUR HUNGER

> "Blessed are they which do hunger and thirst after righteousness: for they shall be filled" (Matthew 5:6).

Your personal spiritual hunger and thirst for more of Jesus and a deeper walk *after* the Spirit will protect you from the deception of religion.

MAINTAIN THE LIBERTY OF THE SPIRIT

> "Stand fast therefore in the liberty wherewith Christ hath made us free, and be not entangled again with the yoke of bondage" (Galatians 5:1).

The religious spirit wants you to become legalistic so it can rob you of your liberty in praise, worship, prayer, and a fervent Christian lifestyle. If you are attending a church that quenches the liberty of the Holy Spirit, then you are probably in a religious church and you are opening yourself up to this murderous spirit. The local church should be a place where you feel free to express your feelings toward the Lord. Never forget, "Where the Spirit of the Lord is — there is liberty" (2 Corinthians 3:17).

PLEASE THE HOLY SPIRIT DAILY

"There is therefore now no condemnation (judgment) to them which are in Christ Jesus, who walk not after the flesh, but after the Spirit" (Romans 8:1).

It's not enough to be in the Spirit. We must aggressively pursue and walk after the Spirit by doing what is pleasing to Him.

STAY AWAY FROM DEAD TRADITIONS

"Making the word of God of none effect through your tradition, which ye have delivered: and many such like things do ye" (Mark 7:13).

Traditions of men try to lock the believer in the past. It doesn't matter how God did things yesterday. What's important is that He still desires to touch His people today. Living in the past is very dangerous. If you're living in the past, then stop! Much of tradition is lifeless and religious churches are dead inside, just like the Pharisees. Our

God is progressive and He seeks to move in new and refreshing ways today.

EXAMINE YOUR MOTIVES

"But as we were allowed of God to be put in trust with the gospel, even so we speak; not as pleasing men, but God, which trieth our hearts" (1 Thessalonians 2:4).

Motive is everything. Who's kingdom are we building? A careful and prayerful examination of our purpose keeps us free from religious activity. Ask yourself this question: "Am I doing good things for the wrong reasons?"

MAINTAIN AN INTIMATE RELATIONSHIP WITH JESUS THROUGH PRAYER

"Confess your faults one to another, and pray one for another, that ye may be healed. The effectual fervent prayer of a righteous man availeth much" (James 5:16).

Prayer is not something one does occasionally, but rather is a lifestyle of fellowship. Maintaining a fervent prayer life is absolutely critical to advancing in your walk with Jesus. If you're lacking here, then you're already a candidate for the religious spirit. Lukewarmness is the number one entryway for the religious spirit.

The religious spirit will always be around, lurking in the darkness and waiting to attack us. But with an awareness of its tactics we can protect ourselves from its corruption. Let's pray...

Dear Jesus, thank You for revealing the attacks from the religious spirit against my perception of Who You are. I love You and desire a deeper, even fuller revelation of Who You are. I submit myself right now to be completely sold out and committed to you. Forgive me my trespasses, sin, arrogance, ignorance, self-righteousness, pride, legalism, false humility, hypocrisy, false motives, control, manipulation, and desire to be admired of men.

Lord, Your Word says that if I confess my sin You are faithful and just to forgive me my sin and cleanse me from all unrighteousness.

Lord, I recognize my lukewarmness and apathetic spiritual condition. Thank You Lord for forgiving me and restoring me. Conform me into Your true image that I might demonstrate Your love, goodness, mercy and the hope of salvation that You have offered to all. Amen.

SCRIPTURAL REFERENCE
TO THE RELIGIOUS SPIRIT

1.) The scribes and Pharisees were hypocrites ready to stone the woman who was caught in the act of adultery, yet there was no mention of stoning the man who was with her.

"And the scribes and Pharisees brought unto him a woman taken in adultery; and when they had set her in the midst, {4} They say unto him, Master, this woman was taken in adultery, in the very act. {5} Now Moses in the law commanded us, that such should be stoned: but what sayest thou? {6} This they said, tempting him, that they might have to accuse him. But Jesus stooped down, and with his finger wrote on the ground, as though he heard them not. {7} So when they continued asking him, he lifted up himself, and said unto them, He that is without sin among you, let him first cast a stone at her. {8} And again he stooped down, and wrote on the ground. {9} And they which heard it, being convicted by their own conscience, went out one by one, beginning at the eldest, even unto the last: and Jesus was left alone, and the woman standing in the midst. {10} When Jesus had lifted up himself, and saw none but the woman, he said unto her, Woman, where are those thine accusers? hath no man condemned thee? {11} She said, No man, Lord. And Jesus said unto her, Neither do I condemn thee: go, and sin no more" (John 8:3-11).

2.) Apostle Peter and Barnabas would not sit and eat with the Gentile believers in Antioch when Jewish brothers came to visit from Jerusalem.

"But when Peter was come to Antioch, I withstood him to the face, because he was to be blamed. {12} For before that certain came from James, he did eat with the Gentiles: but when they were come, he withdrew and separated himself, fearing them which were of the circumcision. {13} And the other Jews dissembled likewise with him; insomuch that Barnabas also was carried away with their dissimulation" (Galatians 2:11-13).

3.) The scribes and Pharisees were legalists who challenged Jesus because His disciples did not wash their hands (ceremonially) before they ate.

"Then came to Jesus scribes and Pharisees, which were of Jerusalem, saying, {2} Why do thy disciples transgress the tradition of the elders? for they wash not their hands when they eat bread. {3} But he answered and said unto them, Why do ye also transgress the commandment of God by your tradition? {4} For God commanded, saying, Honour thy father and mother: and, He that curseth father or mother, let him die the death. {5} But ye say, Whosoever shall say to his father or his mother, It is a gift, by whatsoever thou mightest be profited by me; {6} And honour not his father or his mother, he shall be free. Thus have ye made the commandment of God of no ne effect by your tradition. {7} Ye hypocrites, well did Esaias prophesy of you, saying, {8} This people draweth nigh unto me with their mouth, and honoureth me with their lips; but their heart is far from me. {9} But in vain they do worship me, teaching for doctrines the commandments of men" (Matthew 15:1-9).

4.) Jesus taught His disciples not to pray long prayers like the scribes, who prayed only for show.

"Beware of the scribes, which desire to walk in long robes, and love greetings in the markets, and the highest seats in the synagogues, and the chief rooms at feasts; {47} Which devour widows' houses, and for a show make long prayers: the same shall receive greater damnation" (Luke 20:46-47).

"Woe unto you, scribes and Pharisees, hypocrites! for ye devour widows' houses, and for a pretence (show) make long prayer: therefore ye shall receive the greater damnation" (Matthew 23:14).

5.) Religious spirits are thieves.

"Then Jesus six days before the passover came to Bethany, where Lazarus was which had been dead, whom he raised from the dead. {2} There they made him a supper; and Martha served: but Lazarus was one of them that sat at the table with him. {3} Then took Mary a pound of ointment of spikenard, very costly, and anointed the feet of Jesus, and wiped his feet with her hair: and the house was filled with the odour of the ointment. {4} Then saith one of his disciples, Judas Iscariot, Simon's son, which should betray him, {5} Why was not this ointment sold for three hundred pence, and given to the poor? {6} This he said, not that he cared for the poor; but because he was a thief, and had the bag, and bare what was put therein. {7} Then said Jesus, Let her alone: against the day of my burying hath she kept this. {8} For the poor always ye have with you; but me ye have not always" (John 12:1-8).

6.) A religious council, after a notable miracle and motivated by fear, reprimanded the Apostles Peter and John for speaking the name of Jesus.

"But when they had commanded them to go aside out of the council, they conferred among themselves, {16} Saying, What shall we do to these men? for that indeed a notable miracle hath been done by them is manifest to all them that dwell in Jerusalem; and we cannot deny it. {17} But that it spread no further among the people, let us straitly threaten them, that they speak henceforth to no man in this name. {18} And they called them, and commanded them not to speak at all nor teach in the name of Jesus" (Acts 4:15-18).

7.) When Jesus healed on the Sabbath day that stirred up those with a religious spirit who sought to kill Him.

"And he entered again into the synagogue; and there was a man there which had a withered hand. {2} And they watched him, whether he would heal him on the Sabbath day; that they might accuse him" (Mark 3:1-2). "And the Pharisees went forth, and straightway took counsel with the Herodians against him, how they might destroy him" (Mark 3:6).

"And, behold, there was a woman which had a spirit of infirmity eighteen years, and was bowed together, and could in no wise lift up herself. {12} And when Jesus saw her, he called her to him, and said unto her, Woman, thou art loosed from thine infirmity. {13} And he laid his hands on her: and immediately she was made straight, and glorified God. {14} And the ruler of the synagogue answered with indignation, because that Jesus had healed on the sabbath day, and said unto the people, There are six days in which men ought to work: in them therefore come and be healed, and not on the sabbath day. {15} The Lord then answered him, and said, Thou hypocrite, doth not each one of you on the sabbath loose his ox or his ass from the stall, and lead him away to watering? {16} And ought not this woman, being a daughter of Abraham, whom Satan hath bound, lo, these eighteen years, be loosed from this bond on the sabbath day? {17} And when he had said these things, all his adversaries were ashamed: and all the people rejoiced for all the glorious things that were done by him" (Luke 13:11-17).

8.) Before the fallen Apostle Judas hanged himself he threw the silver pieces paid to him for betraying Jesus into the temple. The chief priests decided it was not legal to put the money back into the treasury because it was blood money. So we learn that these religious spirits could pay for the murder of Jesus with the money but not take the money back.

"When the morning was come, all the chief priests and elders of the people took counsel against Jesus to put him to death: {2} And when they had bound him, they led him away, and delivered him to Pontius Pilate the governor. {3} Then Judas, which had betrayed him, when he saw that he was condemned, repented himself, and brought again the thirty pieces of silver to the chief priests and elders, {4} Saying, I have sinned in that I have betrayed the innocent blood. And they said, What is that to us? see thou to that. {5} And he cast down the pieces of silver in the temple, and departed, and went and hanged himself. {6} And the chief priests took the silver pieces, and said, It is not lawful for to put them into the treasury, because it is the price of blood. {7} And they took counsel, and bought with them the potter's field, to bury strangers in. {8} Wherefore that field was called, The field of blood, unto this day" (Matthew 27:1-8).

9.) When Jesus was taken from Caiaphas, the High Priest, to the building where the Roman governor Pilate stayed, the crowd waited outside and cried out against Jesus. But they would not go inside the building because they might defile themselves and become unclean and be barred from eating the Passover meal. It was OK to cry out, "Crucify him" as long as they didn't enter the building.

"Then led they Jesus from Caiaphas unto the hall of judgment: and it was early; and they themselves went not into the judgment hall, lest they should be defiled; but that they might eat the passover. {29} Pilate then went out unto them, and said, What accusation bring ye against this man? {30} They answered and said unto him, If he were not a malefactor (evil doer), we would not have delivered him up unto thee. {31} Then said Pilate unto them, Take ye him, and judge him according to your law. The Jews therefore said unto him, It is not lawful for us to put any man to death" (John 18:28-31).

10.) Religious spirits desire titles and to be seen (admired) of men.

"But all their works they do for to be seen of men: they make broad their phylacteries, and enlarge the borders of their garments, {6} And love the uppermost rooms at feasts, and the chief seats in the synagogues, {7} And greetings in the markets, and to be called of men, Rabbi, Rabbi" (Matthew 23:5-7).

11.) Religious spirits are hypocrites who say and do not.

"Then spake Jesus to the multitude, and to his disciples, {2} Saying, The scribes and the Pharisees sit in Moses' seat: {3} All therefore whatsoever they bid you observe, that observe and do; but do not ye after their works: for they say, and do not" (Matthew 23:1-3).

12.) Religious spirits will provoke you in an attempt to trap you in your words.

Jesus said, "Woe unto you, lawyers! for ye have taken away the key of knowledge: ye entered not in yourselves, and them that were entering in ye hindered. {53} And as he said these things unto them, the scribes and the Pharisees began to urge him vehemently, and to provoke him to speak of many things: {54} Laying wait for him, and seeking to catch something out of his mouth, that they might accuse him" (Luke 11:52-54).

13.) Religious spirits look good on the outside but inside are very different.

"Woe unto you, scribes and Pharisees, hypocrites! for ye make clean the outside of the cup and of the platter, but within they are full of extortion and excess. {26} Thou blind Pharisee, cleanse first that which is within the cup and platter, that the outside of them may be clean also" (Matthew 23:25-26).

"Woe unto you, scribes and Pharisees, hypocrites! for ye are like unto whited sepulchres, which indeed appear beautiful outward, but are within full of dead men's bones, and of all uncleanness. {28} Even so ye also outwardly appear righteous unto men, but within ye are full of hypocrisy and iniquity" (Matthew 23:27-28).

14.) Religious spirits have a form of godliness but resist the truth.

"Having a form of godliness, but denying the power thereof: from such turn away. {6} For of this sort are they which creep into houses, and lead captive silly women laden with sins, led away with divers lusts, {7} Ever learning, and never able to come to the knowledge of the truth. {8} Now as Jannes and Jambres withstood Moses, so do these also resist the truth: men of corrupt minds, reprobate concerning the faith. {9} But they shall proceed no further: for their folly shall be manifest unto all men, as theirs also was" (2 Timothy 3:5-9).

15.) Religious spirits are murdering spirits.

"Woe unto you, scribes and Pharisees, hypocrites! because ye build the tombs of the prophets, and garnish the sepulchres of the righteous, {30} And say, If we had been in the days of our fathers, we would not have been partakers with them in the blood of the prophets. {31} Wherefore ye be witnesses unto yourselves, that ye are the children of them which killed the prophets. {32} Fill ye up then the measure of your fathers. {33} Ye serpents, ye generation of vipers, how can ye escape the damnation of hell? {34} Wherefore, behold, I send unto you prophets, and wise men, and scribes: and some of them ye shall kill and crucify; and some of them shall ye scourge in your synagogues, and persecute them from city to city" (Matthew 23:29-34).

"Then they cried out with a loud voice, and stopped their ears, and ran upon him with one accord, {58} And cast him (Stephen) out of the city, and stoned him: and the witnesses laid down their clothes at a young man's feet, whose name was Saul" (Acts 7:57-58).

16.) Religious spirits put heavy burdens on others but not themselves.

"For they bind heavy burdens and grievous to be borne, and lay them on men's shoulders; but they themselves will not move them with one of their fingers" (Matthew 23:4).

17.) Religious spirits are legalists.

"Woe unto you, scribes and Pharisees, hypocrites! for ye pay tithe of mint and anise and cummin, and have omitted the weightier matters of the law, judgment, mercy, and faith: these ought ye to have done, and not to leave the other undone. {24} Ye blind guides, which strain (out) a gnat, and swallow a camel" (Matthew 23:23-24).

"As many as desire to make a fair show in the flesh, they constrain you to be circumcised; only lest they should suffer persecution for the cross of Christ. {13} For neither they themselves who are circumcised keep the law; but desire to have you circumcised, that they may glory in your flesh" (Galatians 6:12-13).

INDEX

Trouble 115

U

Unchurched 9
Unloving 39
Unscriptural statements 64
Uppity 55
Usurp authority 62

V

Varieties and flavors 14
Vipers 140
Vows 125

W

Walk after the Spirit 150
Whited sepulcher 143
Wolves 113,142
Words of deception 38
Worship 149
Wrong spirit 23

INVITATION TO DESTINY

Are you hungry for more of God? In addition to preaching the Gospel around the world, we also pastor a powerful, Spirit-filled church in South Florida. The Spirit of God told us to build a church from which to send forth believers that could reach their cities and impact the nations for Jesus Christ.

Have you been searching for God only to find religion? Spirit of Life Ministries (SOLM) is a multi-cultural church where all races gather together in unity and cares for the needs of the whole family. Is something missing from your life? SOLM is a church where you can receive what you need from the Lord. We believe in divine healing, manifesting the gifts of the Spirit, deliverance, restoration, prosperity, finding purpose and making a difference. With God all things are possible.

Are you looking for a place to grow? SOLM is an apostolic church with all five-fold ministry gifts operating. We have a prophetic call and mandate to equip, activate and release every believer into the work of the ministry according to Ephesians 4:11-12. We invite you to come and connect with your destiny and receive confirmation, impartation and activation for your life.

Come adventure with us,
Jonas and Rhonda Clark

SPIRIT OF LIFE MINISTRIES WORLD HEADQUARTERS
27 WEST HALLANDALE BEACH BLVD.
HALLANDALE BEACH, FLORIDA 33009
800.943.6490